PLAY BRIDGE
with Zia

Pupil (learning to play contract bridge). " WHAT IS A PSYCHIC BID ? "

The Expert. " A PSYCHIC BID IS WHEN YOU CALL A SUIT YOU HAVEN'T GOT IN ORDER TO DECEIVE YOUR OPPONENTS INTO THINKING YOU'VE GOT WHAT, UNTIL YOU CALLED, THEY WERE UNDER THE IMPRESSION THEY HAD GOT THEMSELVES."

Cartoon by Leslie Marchant reproduced by permission of *Punch*.

PLAY BRIDGE

with Zia

in collaboration with
Jonathan Rice

BBC BOOKS

Published by BBC Books,
a division of BBC Enterprises Limited
Woodlands, 80 Wood Lane, London W12 0TT
First published 1991
© Zia Mahmood, Jonathan Rice, Gordon Menzies, 1991
ISBN 0 563 36221 9

Designed by David Robinson
Photographs by David Seacombe
Typeset and artworked on AppleMac,
in Monotype Garamond, by David Robinson
Printed and bound in Great Britain by Butler and Tanner Ltd, Frome
Cover printed by Clays Ltd, St Ives Plc

CONTENTS

Zia Mahmood is one of the most popular international bridge players and his successes include medals in several world bridge championships. He was the subject of Channel 4's documentary 'The Ace of Hearts' in 1989 and in 1991 Zia was voted the world's leading bridge player by *Popular Bridge* magazine.

Jonathan Rice is co-author of the best-selling Guinness books of *British Hit Singles*, *British Hit Albums* and *Hits of the Eighties*. He has written several books on cricket, his latest being *The Pavilion Book of Pavilions*.

Bridge has been a part of my life for over thirty years. As a film actor, I find that there are long periods when I have to sit around waiting for something to happen, but at the same time I need to keep my mind active and my concentration sharp. Bridge does all that and more. Indeed, it has proved to be such a stimulating way of filling those stretches of time – which might otherwise have been vast deserts of boredom – that now bridge is the passion of my life. As with acting, it is impossible to reach perfection in bridge, but there is endless enjoyment and stimulation in trying.

I have played bridge with Zia for many years, both as a partner and as an opponent. I am not sure which I enjoy more. Sometimes I wish he was partnering somebody else when an overbid contract fails, and on other occasions his unconventional but ruthlessly planned and executed defence has meant disaster for what I had thought to be a perfectly safe contract. His style of play is flamboyant while mine is more conservative, but the brilliance of his best ideas is unforgettable. And he makes bridge fun.

Zia is one of the great players of bridge, and he is also one of the great communicators of his enthusiasm for the game, and the excitement that it can generate. I am very pleased that Zia has seized this opportunity to make bridge more widely understood and appreciated and this book, *Play Bridge With Zia*, will give you hours of real pleasure.

Omar Sharif

CHAPTER 1

AN INTRODUCTION TO BRIDGE

A few months ago fifteen hundred people sat in a vast hotel room in Toronto, Canada, in almost total silence. Suddenly, fire alarm bells started going off in all directions. But nobody moved. There was no panic, no hysteria and no mad rush for the exits. Apart from a few irritated looks and turned heads, nobody paid the bells any attention. Why? Because the fifteen hundred people were involved in a bridge tournament, and it takes more than a little thing like a hotel fire to break their concentration at a time like that. Not even an avalanche or an earthquake could move a bridge player when he is competing in a tournament, so what chance did a mere fire have?

Yet, the three million of us in Britain and the one hundred million people around the world who have been initiated into its mysteries, seem crazy to those who do not play bridge, childishly fiddling with little bits of cardboard all day and all night. Those who think the word finesse means the proper way to hold a knife and fork, that pass is what you try to do with a pretty girl at a dinner party, or that squeeze is a term used by a wrestling commentator or the Chancellor of the Exchequer, will think that bridge players are not only crazy but boring with it. Well, maybe that is the popular image of bridge, but before I was a bridge player, I used to be an accountant, so I ought to know about boring, and believe me bridge is not boring. I'm sure there are many of you reading this book who play cards already, maybe blackjack or poker, which you think must be far more exciting than bridge. Well, I used to think so too. Now I play blackjack and poker to relax and unwind after the excitement and tension of a bridge session. Bridge players may be crazy, but we like our craziness, and by the time you have finished reading this book, I hope you too will be just a bit crazier about this wonderful and fascinating game.

The first good thing about bridge is that you need no expensive equipment to get started. Forget the cost of a set of golf clubs, or the latest graphite tennis racket; for bridge all you need is three other people, a pack of cards and a pencil and paper to keep score. Some people would say that a stout pair of footballer's shinpads are a useful accessory, but a good bridge partner does not need the added encouragement of a sharp kick beneath the table.

PARTNERSHIP

Bridge is a partnership game. At the start of a session, the four players cut the pack for partners. The two players who cut the highest cards partner each other, as do the two who picked the lowest cards. The cards are ranked with the aces high, down to the two at the bottom. The denominations or suits, are ranked, by coincidence, in reverse alphabetical order, with spades as the highest ranked, followed by hearts, diamonds and finally the lowest ranking suit clubs. So the seven of spades, for example, outranks the seven of hearts, and the jack of diamonds would beat the jack of clubs if both cards were cut in the search for partners.

The partners sit opposite each other, in positions which are designated by the four points of the compass. Thus, North partners South and East partners West. The player who cut the highest card has the choice of seat and deals first. The jokers are not used, so a pack of cards for bridge consists of 52 cards, which are dealt face down, clockwise, beginning with the player on the dealer's left. Once all the cards have been dealt, each player picks up his pile of cards, which is called a hand, and sorts it into suits. At this point it is worth counting your cards. You are supposed to have 13 each, but I have played in competitions where through some simple mistake one player had 12 or 14 cards, and did not notice until the bidding was over and the play of the hand had started. I've done it myself.

A typical deal may turn out something like this:

**A TIP FROM
OMAR SHARIF**

'The first and most important tip I have for a bridge player is to be courteous and to make your partner feel comfortable – for the very simple reason that the more your partner feels comfortable, the better he will perform. So try even before you start the game to make him feel good. Make him feel self-confident, and don't make too many remarks to your partner about his game. It will only make him play worse.'

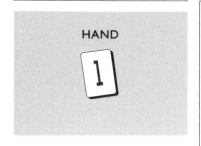

HAND

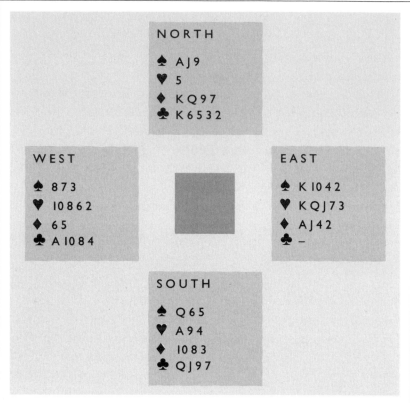

NORTH
♠ A J 9
♥ 5
♦ K Q 9 7
♣ K 6 5 3 2

WEST
♠ 8 7 3
♥ 10 8 6 2
♦ 6 5
♣ A 10 8 4

EAST
♠ K 10 4 2
♥ K Q J 7 3
♦ A J 4 2
♣ –

SOUTH
♠ Q 6 5
♥ A 9 4
♦ 10 8 3
♣ Q J 9 7

East was dealt no clubs at all. This is known as a void, and has its advantages as we shall see. North has only one heart, which is called a singleton. West finds himself with only two diamonds, a doubleton. South holds at least three of every suit and so has a balanced hand. West's hand is also balanced, a description given to all hands with three or four cards in three suits and no more than one doubleton. The only other distribution of cards which is called a balanced hand is one where there are five cards in one suit, three in two other suits and one doubleton. These types of hand are the most common.

Assuming that you have the right number of cards and that you have sorted them successfully into suits, the next question you will ask is, what is the purpose of the game? Well, in simple terms it is for you and your partner to win as many tricks as you can. A trick consists of four cards, one contributed by each player, so that a total of 13 tricks are available to be won on each hand. The player who wins a trick leads the first card of the next trick, face up, and the other three players follow in clockwise order around the table. The player who plays the highest card of the suit led wins the trick. Each player is obliged to follow the suit of the first card played, if he can. If he cannot, he has the choice of throwing away any card from his hand onto the trick, or of ruffing (playing a trump). A trump card is a card from a suit that, for the purposes of that particular contract, ranks higher than any other suit. The contract and therefore the ranking of the suits in that contract is decided at the auction (see page 12). Let us assume, for example that you are in North's seat in the hand just dealt, and that clubs are trumps.

You hold:

♠ A J 9   ♥ 5   ♦ K Q 9 7   ♣ K 6 5 3 2

If West leads the ten of hearts, you must put your five of hearts on the trick, even though it will not, of course, win. Let us suppose that you were the fourth to play, and that your partner, South, won the trick by playing his ace of hearts. He will collect up the four cards and put them face down in front of him on the table. If on the next trick your partner leads another heart, you will have the choice of playing a club when your turn comes round, as clubs are trumps, or of discarding a diamond or a spade. Even if you discarded the ace of spades, the mightiest card in the pack, it could not win the trick, although the lowly two of clubs would because it is a trump. What you actually should play will depend on many factors, which we shall come to a little later. For the time being, just remember that you must always follow suit if you can. Failure to follow suit when you can is known as revoking, and the penalty is to transfer two tricks from the guilty partnership to the other side (or only one if the trick on which the revoke occurred was lost by the revoking pair anyway). The penalty for revoking is enough to turn a potentially winning partnership into a losing one.

However, the partnership that wins the most tricks does not necessarily win the hand. It is not like football (even if you are wearing those shinpads) where the side that scores more goals wins. In bridge we do not merely say, 'We won eight tricks, they won five. So we are the winners'. In bridge, you have to do what you said you would do at the auction in order to win the hand.

THE AUCTION

The auction decides the contract. The contract is the number of tricks in any one suit that one or other partnership says it will make. To decide the contract all players bid at the auction for the right to name the trump suit by agreeing, or contracting, in partnership, to make a certain number of tricks with that suit as trumps. The partnership that bids to make the highest number of tricks buys the contract and the contract is played with that partnership's named suit as trumps. The auction is what separates bridge from most other forms of card game, although the principle of the auction is not unique to bridge. At a Saturday morning auction for second hand furniture, if you really want that 1920s flower vase, you have to offer more for it than anybody else. So in bridge, if you really want the contract, you and your partner have to be prepared to pledge to buy more tricks than your opponents.

The bidding begins with the dealer, and passes clockwise round the table. However, there is one small snag: the auction in bridge is not conducted in plain English. It is conducted in the language of bridge which has very few words, (the only words allowed are One, Two, Three, Four, Five, Six, Seven, Spades, Hearts, Diamonds, Clubs, No Trumps, Double, Redouble and Pass or No Bid) but they have to convey a mountain of meaning, and it is here that confusion arises for the beginner. However, if you bear in mind that the point of the bidding process is for you and your partner to tell each other which is your best suit, and how many tricks you think you can make with that suit as trumps, then a lot of the complications fall away.

A bid takes the form of a number and a denomination, for example One Club. This does not mean you reckon you can win one trick with clubs as trumps. That would be too easy. Before any bidding begins, it is assumed that the buyers of the contract will take at least six tricks, which is known as the book. The book is added to the number of tricks bid and therefore One Club means that the bidder thinks he and his partner can make 6+1 tricks with clubs as trumps. Seven Clubs would mean that the partnership believes it can make all 13 tricks if clubs are trumps.

You will remember that the suits are ranked in reverse alphabetical order — spades, hearts, diamonds and clubs. You can, if you prefer, decide to play with no suit nominated as trumps, in which case you would bid in No Trumps. No Trumps are ranked higher than spades. So, for example, a bid of One Heart is a higher bid than One Club, and would win the auction if those were the only two bids. Two Clubs, on the other hand, beats One Heart or even One No Trump. The bidding progresses round the table beginning with the dealer, and continues until a bid is followed by three consecutive Pass or No Bid calls. If all four hands pass at their first turn, the hand is 'passed out' and redealt. Each new bid must, of course, be higher than the one before. Unlike that Saturday morning auction where you are hoping to secure the 1920s vase, however, you are not bidding against everybody else in the room. You are bidding with your partner against the other partnership, and the purpose of the bidding is to end up with a contract which your side is most happy with. In other words, what can the combined strength of your 26 cards achieve?

THE LANGUAGE OF BIDDING

The only problem in reaching the right contract is that you are not allowed to look at each other's cards and you are not allowed to use any other words except the ones I mentioned earlier. You cannot say to your partner, 'I've got six hearts but no diamonds at all. What about you?' The only way you can convey that message, or something like it, is by the use of the bidding language, which like all languages has meaning beyond the simple message of the words. The man who scratches his nose or tugs on his earlobe when you are bidding for that vase is using the language of the auction room to try to beat you to that particular treasure, yet his meaning is clear to most people in the room. We shall deal in greater detail with the way to use the language of the bridge auction in the next chapter, but for the time being all you have to remember is that the bids are a conversation between you and your partner about the relative strengths and weaknesses of your hands.

And, of course, the opposing partners also talk to each other in the language of bidding, and listen to your bids, so that it is possible for a skilful bidder to learn a great deal about all the hands held before a single card is played.

Let us imagine you have been dealt the following hand:

♠ Q 5 4 3   ♥ A 8 3   ♦ A K J 10 5   ♣ 5

After adding up your points (see Chapter Two), you think you can take seven tricks if diamonds are trumps. So you might open the bidding by saying One Diamond. Now what would your partner do if he held the following hand?:

♠ 10 7 2   ♥ K J 10 9 7   ♦ 8 6   ♣ A 6 4

Well, he should look at his diamonds and think, 'Not a lot of support I can give my partner with only two little cards in his suit. All the same, he has opened the bidding, so I want to say something to show that we can make a contract. My hearts are pretty good. Why don't I try them?' So your partner might sum up all those thoughts in the simple bid, One Heart.

At this point, you can look at your cards and think, 'Well, partner has bid hearts. I've got three, including the ace, so let's agree on hearts as the suit to play in.' That message is translated to your partner in the two words, Two Hearts. You have agreed which suit to play as trumps. This bid has increased the number of tricks you have committed to make, but you are confident about saying your partnership can now make eight tricks because of what your partner has told you about the strength of his hand. If his hearts had been totally unacceptable to you, you would not have been able to go back to One Diamond, or even to switch to One Club. You would have had to go higher, One Spade or Two Diamonds. Unless you Pass, each bid must take the partnership higher up the bidding ladder, and if the opposing side are bidding as well, their bids must also increase the stakes each time. So if West had decided he wanted to bid after your partner had said One Heart, he would have had to bid at least One Spade. If clubs were his preferred suit, he would have to start at Two Clubs. The two sides compete in the same auction, for the same prize, so the bids have to get higher at each bid from either partnership.

Let us assume in this case, however, that the opposition have not bid at all. The bidding will have gone like this:

NORTH	EAST	SOUTH	WEST
(You)		(Partner)	
1 ♦	PASS	1 ♥	PASS
2 ♥	PASS	PASS	PASS

You and your partner have bought the contract, which is to win, or make, eight tricks, (6+2), with hearts as trumps. If you manage to make at least eight tricks, your partnership has made the contract. If you fail, then East-West has defeated the contract. Of course, the bidding could in theory go on up as far as Seven No Trumps, which is the highest possible contract, implying that the partnership will make all thirteen tricks (6+7) with no suit as trumps. To be confident of this, your partnership would have to have all four aces plus most of the kings, queens, jacks, etc., so it is a rare bid. Bidding and winning all the tricks is known as a grand slam, while bidding and winning twelve tricks is known as a small slam.

East-West are said to be the Defenders in our Two Hearts contract. On your side, North-South, the team will consist of a Declarer and a Dummy. The Declarer will play both hands, and the one who ends up being Dummy can potter off and make a cup of coffee or watch the end of the news on the television. What he cannot do is help the Declarer play the hand, except to warn him if he is about to lead a card from the wrong hand, or to revoke.

DECLARER AND DUMMY

But who is Declarer and who is Dummy? The rule is simple. Declarer is the partner who first bid the denomination which ended up becoming the trump suit, and his partner is Dummy. So in this case, you become Dummy because it was your partner who first bid hearts, the suit in which the contract is to be played. The fact that it was you who made the first bid of One Diamond, and that it was you who set the final level of the contract with your bid of Two Hearts is neither here nor there. You are Dummy and your partner is Declarer. The first thing that happens in the play of the hand is that the Defender on the left of Declarer (in this case West), leads the first card, at which point Dummy puts all his cards on the table. The cards are traditionally laid out with the trump suit arranged on the left as Declarer views it, on Dummy's right. From this point on, Declarer plays both hands in his attempt to make the contract. He now has a chance to look at both hands and decide how he is going to make the eight tricks he has contracted. The defence also has the chance to look at Dummy and note its strengths and weaknesses as they attempt to take the six tricks which will be needed to defeat the contract.

SCORING

However, let us suppose that by a combination of subtle bidding, clever card play and sheer beginner's luck, you make the contract, and even manage one extra trick. What have you scored? The full details of the scoring system are included from page 118, but here you need to know that the primary object is to score 100 points to make a game. These 100 points can be collected either in one hand, by bidding high enough and then making the contract, or gradually over two or more hands. Points are awarded for every trick in a successful contract beyond the book of six tricks. The points awarded also vary according to the denomination in which the contract was played. Twenty points are awarded for every trick in club or diamond contracts (known as the minor suits) and 30 points are awarded for every trick in heart or spade contracts (known as the major suits). Thus, you will see that a contract of Four Hearts or Four Spades will give you game if achieved ($4 \times 30 = 120$ points), but it will take a contract of Five Clubs or Five Diamonds to get to the magic figure of 100 points. Contracts in No Trumps are scored slightly differently again, with 40 points being awarded for the first trick above book, and 30 points for each succeeding trick. Thus a contract of just Three No Trumps ($40+30+30=100$) will give you game, and that is why this is the most commonly bid contract.

Now, to add to the fun, or to make you more confused than you already are, the scoresheet is divided by a line above or below which the scores are entered. It is the score below the line which has to reach 100 points to make a game, and the only points that are entered below the line are the points marking the progress of the partnerships towards game. You may only score tricks which have been both bid and made below the line. Overtricks are tricks made but not bid. Undertricks are tricks bid but not made. Above the line, points are entered for overtricks, undertricks, (points are awarded to the Defence if the Declarer fails to make the contract) and bonuses for slams, games, honours (the five highest ranking cards in a suit which merit a score only if they are the trump suit's honours) and the like. So in the contract we have just made, Two Hearts with one overtrick, the score would show 60 points below the line (30+30) and 30 more above the line, for the overtrick. If we had bid Three Hearts, all 90 points would have gone below the line, almost giving us game, or 100 points.

If we had failed to make the contract, say taking only seven tricks and thus going what is known as one down, we would have scored no points above or below the line, but our opponents would have scored a penalty against us of 50 points (the rate per non-vulnerable undertrick regardless of the denomination of the contract) above the line. All these scores are made greater by doubling, redoubling or by the side which failed being vulnerable. If you do not think your opponents have any chance of making the contract bid, you have the option of saying Double when it is your turn to bid, which has the effect of increasing the points at stake. If your opponent is sure he *can* make the contract bid, he has the option of saying Redouble, which gears up the points being played for still further. A partnership becomes vulnerable when it has won one game (100 points) in the rubber (the best of three games). A vulnerable partnership that goes down in an attempt to make a contract gives their opponents roughly double the score above the line that they would make if the partnership were not vulnerable. A vulnerable partnership that bid a slam, was not believed and thus was doubled, and then went six tricks down, would find its opponents with a score of 1700 points above the line, significantly more than any bonus they might win for taking the game or the rubber, or indeed for making the slam themselves. The bonuses awarded for making a doubled contract, for holding all five honours (A K Q J 10) in the trump suit and so on, like all points scored above the line, do not count towards game. They are merely added up at the end of the rubber to see which partnership has won the most points. It is possible to win the rubber, but score fewer points in total than your opponents, just as in tennis it is possible to win fewer points but more games, or to win fewer games but more sets. So the method of scoring has a significant effect on the tactics of the bidding and the play, and it is as well for all players to be thoroughly familiar with the scoring before venturing too deeply into the mysteries of bridge. But don't worry too much if the scoring confuses you at this stage. The more you play the quicker you will understand the scoring.

THE ETHICS OF BRIDGE

The method of physically playing the cards does not require any great lessons, and we will not waste space with full colour photographs showing how to hold the cards. It requires no particular skill, and although there have been many books written on the most obscure aspects of bridge, there has never been much written about how to hold the cards, except to say that their faces should be kept hidden from all the other players. However, do avoid the annoying habit of constantly moving the cards about in your hand as you prepare to play them, and of fingering them more than is necessary. Any excessive fidgeting with your cards could be interpreted as an unauthorised signal to your partner, which is completely unacceptable.

Before we go any further into the structure and tactics of the game, it is worth remembering some really good advice I was given at the beginning of my bridge career, and which is still absolutely fundamental to successful bridge. A lot of beginners are so involved in learning the mechanics of the game that they are not taught the importance of the ethics. It is very important to try to bid and to play in an even tempo and without visible or audible emotion. Emphasis or intonation when bidding, or exaggerated body language at any stage of the game, is unethical, which in bridge is almost as strong a word as cheating. So do not laugh, grimace, fidget or sigh sadly as you look despairingly towards the heavens. This is not allowed. Play fairly and as evenly as possible. It is much more important to be thought of as a scrupulously honest player than to win. This is the first quality of all the great players. Now you are ready to play.

CHAPTER

2

This Joker card appears throughout the book where more advanced play is described.

THE VALUE OF YOUR HAND AND THE BASICS OF BIDDING

HIGH CARD POINTS

As we have seen, once the cards have been dealt, the playing of the hand begins with the auction. The players have to tell their partners, using the language of bridge, called bidding, something about the character of the hand they have been dealt. How strong is my hand? Are there any suits which are particularly long or strong? Can I contribute to a winning partnership? Basically each player should describe the contents of his hand as accurately as possible.

But how do we learn the language of the auction? How do we learn when to bid and when to pass? When you learn a foreign language, it is easy to pick up a few new words, but unless you know what they mean and when to use them, you are likely to make a whole lot of mistakes. It is no good being able to say *bonjour* in French if you have no idea what it means or when to use it. In bridge, it is all very well knowing that One Club is something bridge players sometimes say when they bid, but how do they know when a One Club hand comes along? What if I say One Club when I ought to have said Three Spades or Pass? It might as well be *bonsoir* and goodnight.

Well, the good thing about the language of bridge is that it is logical. There are not too many irregular verbs to worry about and the vocabulary is very limited. The cornerstone of the grammar of bidding for all beginners is the point count. If you are trying to tell your partner something about your hand, then the first thing to discover is how to let yourself know something about your hand.

This is where the point count comes in. What you want your cards to do for you is to win tricks, so you need to be able to assess the trick taking power of your hand. By far the most commonly used way of doing this is by allocating points to the cards you hold which can win tricks for you. As the cards which are most likely to win tricks are the highest ones, we simply apply the magic formula of four points for every ace, three points for every king, two for each queen and one for the jacks. This means that there are a total of 40 high card points in every deal (4+3+2+1=10 per suit, × 4 suits = 40), so an average hand would contain 10 points. If you have more than 10 points, then you can consider that you have a better than average hand. With this information, you have made the transition from card player to bridge player, and it may well be time to enter the auction.

Consider these three hands:

♠ A K Q 7   ♥ A 4 3   ♦ 1 0 8 2   ♣ 7 5 2

♠ A K Q 9 7 4   ♥ A 3   ♦ 2   ♣ 1 0 8 7 5 and

♠ A K Q J 1 0 9 8 7 6 5 4 3 2   ♥ –   ♦ –   ♣ –

Using the point count system, we can see that the first two hands contain 13 high card points, four for the aces, three for the kings and two for the queens, while the third hand only contains 10 high card points. There is no hard and fast rule for opening the bidding, either as the first to bid the hand or the first in your partnership to bid, but it is generally accepted that you need at least 12 high card points. If your partner has already bid, you can reply as long as the value of your hand is at least six high card points. But are the three hands above really of equal value? Which would you rather play with?

If you said the third of the three hands, well done. If you hold all the cards in one suit and that suit becomes trumps, you would know for sure that you would win every trick, so the third hand is worth a great deal more than the other two hands shown here, despite the fact that it only has 10 high card points and the other two hands have 13 high card points each. Counting points is very valuable, but repeated from page 21

♠ A K Q 7
♥ A 4 3
♦ 1 0 8 2
♣ 7 5 2

♠ A K Q 9 7 4
♥ A 3
♦ 2
♣ 1 0 8 7 5

♠ A K Q J 1 0 9 8 7 6 5 4 3 2
♥ –
♦ –
♣ –

if you have a hand with suits of widely varying lengths, then you need to give yourself some value for the distribution of the cards as well.

LENGTH POINTS

The rule applied to the value of a hand by its length is straightforward. Given that most hands will contain suits mainly of two, three or four cards each, extra points are given for every suit of five cards or more. For a five-card suit, one point is given, for a six-card suit two points, for a seven-card suit three points and for an eight-card suit four points. So if we go back to the three hands on page 21, we see that the first hand, which contains three three-card suits and one four-card suit, does not pick up any extra value for the length of the suits, or distribution. It is a balanced hand. The second hand, on the other hand, contains six spades. That means we can award ourselves a further two points for distribution, bringing the total value of our hand to 15 points, a rather better total than the first hand. Some players award themselves one point for each card in excess of four in any one suit, so that if, as in the third hand, they hold all 13 spades, they would give themselves nine length points, making a total point count of 90.

One word of warning about length points. Unlike high card points, there is no fixed number of total length points which will be awarded after any deal. We know that there will always be 40 high card points to be divided up between the four players, but there is no such mathematical certainty with length points. It could be that all four players have balanced hands, so that nobody awards himself any length points. There could be, in an extreme case, four six card suits and four seven card suits in play, which means that a total of 20 length points could be awarded. In the unlikely event of a perfect deal (mathematically virtually impossible but in practice we seem to hear about them surprisingly often) in which each player receives 13 cards in one suit, there would be 36 length points (9×4) to go with the 40 high card points. Because you do not know exactly how many length points are being counted in any auction, be very careful if your point count is more dependent on length than on high cards.

DUMMY POINTS

Remember that bridge is a partnership game. You need to try to work out how many combined points you and your partner hold between you, and whether they are enough to reach a makeable contract.

Consider this hand:

♠ A 9 5 3 2   ♥ –   ♦ A Q 8 6 5 3   ♣ K 7

If you were planning to open the bidding, you would count your high card points, and get the answer thirteen, and your length points, one in spades and two in diamonds, and reach the total of 16. Plenty for an opening bid. But what if your partner had dealt and had already opened the bidding? Say he had bid One Spade, what then? You love spades too, so the contract could well be in spades, which will make you Dummy. Is your hand worth the same if it is Dummy as if you are bidding to be Declarer or defending your opponents' contract?

The answer is no. That void in hearts will be a godsend to your partner, and you need to allocate some value to it, which means we need a way of evaluating a hand which may well end up as Dummy. But what if partner had opened the bidding with One Heart? You would do your best to put him off that disastrous course by bidding almost anything else, but if he decides he must play in hearts, then your hand as Dummy is not going to be much use to him. You need to take notice of every possibility and give your hand a valuation accordingly.

Dummy Points are used when you think you are going to be Dummy, and when you support your partner's choice of trumps. If the contract is to be in spades, then you need to put a value on your shortage of hearts which will allow him to make tricks with some of your small trumps when hearts are played. Dummy points put a value on a void of five points, three points on a singleton and one point on a doubleton. So in this hand, in response to One Spade bid, you would revalue your hand as being worth 13 high card points plus five Dummy points for the void and one point for the doubleton club, making a total of 19 points. If your partner had opened One Heart, you could not support his

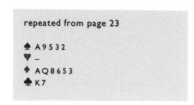

repeated from page 23

♠ A9532
♥ –
♦ AQ8653
♣ K7

HAND

2

bid, for hearts would be the trump suit. You would value your hand differently at 16 points (13 high card points plus 3 for length), and hope you could persuade your partner that hearts was not the best suit for your partnership in this hand.

OPENING THE BIDDING

Now that you know how to value your hand you must decide when to say Pass and when to venture onto the auction ladder and bid for a contract. Given that you need at least 12 high card points in your hand before you launch yourself into the auction, consider this hand:

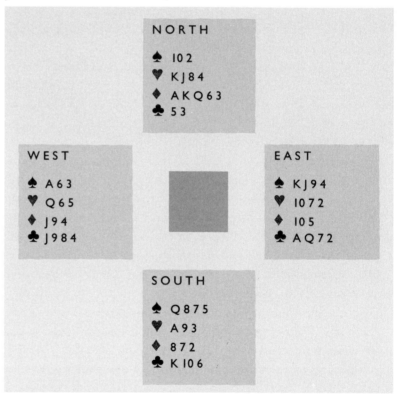

NORTH
♠ 10 2
♥ K J 8 4
♦ A K Q 6 3
♣ 5 3

WEST
♠ A 6 3
♥ Q 6 5
♦ J 9 4
♣ J 9 8 4

EAST
♠ K J 9 4
♥ 10 7 2
♦ 10 5
♣ A Q 7 2

SOUTH
♠ Q 8 7 5
♥ A 9 3
♦ 8 7 2
♣ K 10 6

West was the dealer, so he has the chance to make the opening bid. But he counts up his points and realises he has only eight high card points, and no extra points for length, so there is nothing he can sensibly bid. If his partner says something, then he may well be able to make a bid on the next round to back him up, but there is not enough strength in West's own hand for an opening bid. So he says Pass.

North, the next person to have the chance to bid in the clockwise auction, has counted her points and realises she has 13 high card points, plus an extra point for her length in diamonds. Fourteen points is enough to open the bidding, and first of all she wants to let her partner know about her best suit, diamonds. Notice that although North has high cards in her long suit, diamonds, it is the *length* rather than the strength which is the key when deciding which suit to bid. One Diamond is the bid. East has been studying his cards, but with only 10 high card points and nothing extra for length, he sees no possibility of making a bid, especially as his partner did not open the bidding and is therefore unlikely to be any stronger than he is. If between them they have 20 points, that is still not enough to make a game contract, especially as his distribution is so balanced. So he too says Pass.

The auction is now likely to be dominated by the North-South partnership. South looks at her cards, and although she only has nine points, that is enough for a reply, because she knows that her partner must have at least 12 or 13 to make an opening bid in a suit so that between them they have 22 points or more. However, diamonds are her weakest suit, so although she has three which may help her partner, she really ought to mention her spades which is her strongest suit. There is no point in bidding higher than necessary, and as spades outrank diamonds, she can safely bid One Spade so that the partnership at this stage still only expects to make book plus one trick (6+1).

West passes again, and North, on hearing spades, thinks, 'Well, my partner may well have a particularly strong hand because she only nudged us into spades without committing to take any more tricks.' A possible reply which tells your partner that you too have a good hand (at least 15 high card points) is called a jump bid, (a bid two levels higher). Because South did not jump, North suspects that her own hand is the stronger hand, but she does not like spades. If South has any support for her diamonds, they will be better off in that suit. She bids Two Diamonds.

East passes again, and South has to make a decision. 'North obviously likes diamonds a whole lot more than spades. I have three small diamonds, which will support my partner if diamonds are trumps. I could, perhaps, bid my clubs or my hearts, but that looks dangerous for two reasons. Both those suits only have three cards and I know that three card suits should not be bid except when raising a bid of the same suit, and also if I bid clubs I will have to raise the level and we might end up in a Three Diamond contract which may be a little too high for us, considering that my partner's minimum rebid suggests that she does not have a great hand. All in all I think I had better not say anything more.' South passes, as does West, making three consecutive passes. So the auction is over. The North-South partnership has contracted to win eight tricks with diamonds as trumps, a makeable contract in my opinion.

Now take a look at this hand:

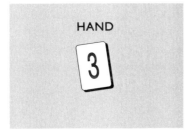

HAND
3

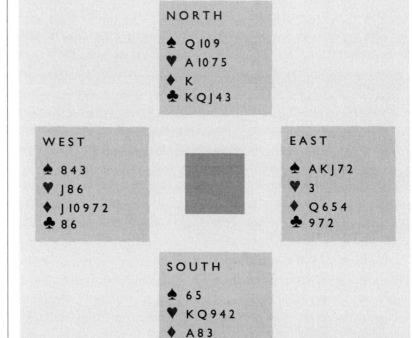

NORTH
♠ Q 10 9
♥ A 10 7 5
♦ K
♣ K Q J 4 3

WEST
♠ 8 4 3
♥ J 8 6
♦ J 10 9 7 2
♣ 8 6

EAST
♠ A K J 7 2
♥ 3
♦ Q 6 5 4
♣ 9 7 2

SOUTH
♠ 6 5
♥ K Q 9 4 2
♦ A 8 3
♣ A 10 5

East dealt and has the opportunity to open the bidding, but with only ten points decides to pass. South has a good hand, suitable for a One No Trump bid. She has a balanced hand and 13 high card points. If you hold a balanced hand and if you have between 12 and 14 high card points, then you should bid One No Trump. You can also use a One No Trump opening to show 15 to 17 high card points. It is a matter of personal style and preference. I prefer a weak no trump, as in South's hand. South bid One No Trump, although few would criticise the alternative opening bid of One Heart.

West has a stinker. Two jacks, giving two high card points, and a third point for the length of his string of five diamonds. But with three points, not even I would venture into the bidding. North, on the other hand, likes what he hears. His partner has bid One No Trump, which means that she must have at least 12 points and a balanced hand. With North's 15 high card points, that means they must have at least 27 points between them, not to mention the length point for the five clubs. He bids Two Clubs, which could be a way of showing his clubs, or it could be a way of asking South to suggest a compatible major suit. The second way of interpreting this bid is known as a conventional bid: a bid which means more than the simple message initially conveyed by the number and suit bid. This particular convention is the Stayman Convention and is explained in detail on page 34.

East has to pass, despite his attractive spade suit: he has no reason to enter an auction where his opponents seem to have all the values.

South correctly interprets the Two Clubs bid as a conventional bid asking for a major suit. She suggests her hearts. Two Hearts. West passes again.

North thinks, 'Partner has shown her major suit by saying Two Hearts and I have a fit for hearts. So I will try Three Hearts.' Which he does.

When I watched my pupils bidding this hand, they got as far as Three Hearts. The hand was played, and North-South made their contract easily. There is nothing wrong with making a contract which brings in 90 points below the line, but it was a pity they did not find their way to a contract which would have brought them in 120 points and game. The cards were there, but the conversation did not disclose them. Where did they go wrong?

THE THREE ZONES – PARTSCORE, GAME & SLAM

What happened here was that once South had told North

A TIP FROM
OMAR SHARIF

'When you are in doubt
about whether to bid into
the slam zone or not,
remember to look at the
two keys of slam bidding
– your trumps and your
controls. To make a slam
you need good trump
quality and you need
good controls (aces, kings
or a shortage in a suit
other than trumps).
Without these, it is not
wise to move into the
slam zone. Be content to
stop at game.'

that she had 12 to 14 points and a balanced hand (by opening One No Trump), North should have taken the initiative. He should have seen that with South's minimum of 12 points, their combined total of at least 27 points was enough to take them to a game. He would have known this if he had been aware of the three zones.

Allow me to digress for a moment. I was taking some shirts to be dry cleaned the other day when the lady behind the counter suddenly said, 'How do you stop?' This rather perplexed me as I had no idea what she was talking about. 'How do you stop?' she repeated and continued before I could leave my shirts and run. 'How do you bring the auction to a close at the right level?' That, of course, is the million dollar question, and not even I can get it right every time. Sometimes I get stuck in a contract which is too optimistic to make, and at other times, as we have just seen with North-South in Three Hearts, we stop short of our goal. Getting to the right level contract reminds me of the story of the man who jumped off a fifty storey skyscraper. As he fell past each floor the people in the building could hear him saying, 'So far, so good.' Yes, so far so good, but he still made an awful mess on the pavement at the end of his journey. The secret of successful bidding is not to make an awful mess at the end. That means getting to the right level, no higher and no lower. Simple? Yes and no.

To try to prevent that messy ending, it helps to decide which one of three zones is the right one for the combined strength of a partnership. The zones are called the *partscore zone*, the *game zone* and the *slam zone*. Remembering that the total high card point count possible is 40, if you as a pair have fewer than 26 points, then any contract you reach should probably be in the partscore zone. That means you should not aim higher than a contract which will take you just part of the way to your target of 100 points below the line, such as One Club which will bring in just 20 points, or Two Hearts which earns 60 points. If you and your partner have between 26 and 32 points, then you are in the game zone and you should be bidding game. Contracts of Three No Trumps, Four Hearts, Four Spades, Five Clubs or Five Diamonds are the game scores, because if you make them successfully, you will have at least the magic 100 below the line for game. Bob Hamman, the great American bridge player, has even been quoted as saying that all game bids stop at Three No Trumps, because that is the easiest game contract to make. And that's true as a general rule for game contracts. The third zone is the most enjoyable one. It deals with the big hands. If between you, you can boast at least 33 points, then you are in the slam zone and stopping at Three No Trumps would be unadventurous. With 33 to 36 points, a small slam ought to be possible. If you have 37 or over, then head for a grand slam.

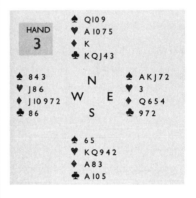

Let us look at that last hand again. South bid One No Trump. North now knew that her partner held between 12 and 14 high card points, so she should have added these points to her own, and realised that the partnership held a total of between 27 and 29 high card points, which puts them into the game zone. North correctly enquired of South whether she had four or more cards in hearts or spades (using the Stayman Convention) and South bid Two Hearts, showing that she held at least four hearts which would bring the total hearts held by the partnership to eight, or possibly more. North's actual choice of Three Hearts left South not knowing whether to bid Four Hearts and try for game – which in any event I think she should have done. The second member of a partnership (the Responder) to bid generally knows more about the combined hands than the first bidder, and so should take the lead and act as captain, so to speak. If the Responder does not act boldly, the partnership may drift. Here North *knew* that the partnership should play game in hearts – no more, no less – so it was his duty to bid Four Hearts himself. At that point South would have passed, and they would have cruised home in style.

Bidding a slam relies on a mixture of the rules and on the feel and distribution of the cards. There is one basic general rule, however, which says that if you are going for a grand slam, you probably need to have 37 or more points, because you cannot afford for the defence to have even one ace. An ace counts four high card points, so if you and your partner have 37, the defence cannot have more than three, which means they have no aces. This is a case where length points have to be included with extreme caution. If you have a void, then the ace of that suit in an

HAND

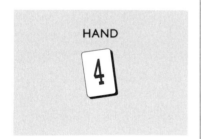

opponent's hand is less important because it can be ruffed. So an eight card suit in your hand is probably as valuable as that last ace, which is why they would both be awarded four points. But if you are going for a grand slam, it is certainly better to have the high card points, and hope for a little helpful distribution as well. Of course, if the contract is Seven No Trumps, there is no chance of ruffing any stray aces. A no trump contract usually implies balanced hands, and the need for the partnership to hold all four aces is paramount.

Little slams are more vague in their requirements, although we have already established that as a guideline, the partnership hoping to win twelve tricks ought to hold between 33 and 36 high card points.

But remember point count is only a guide. Distribution has its own laws and often ignores point count.

Consider this hand:

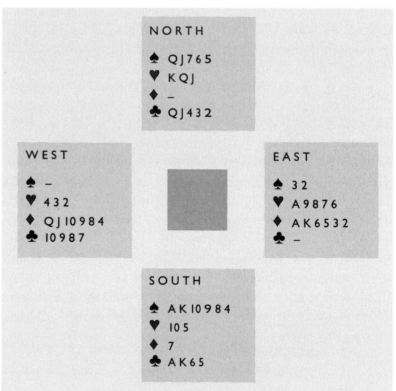

NORTH
♠ Q J 7 6 5
♥ K Q J
♦ –
♣ Q J 4 3 2

WEST
♠ –
♥ 4 3 2
♦ Q J 10 9 8 4
♣ 10 9 8 7

EAST
♠ 3 2
♥ A 9 8 7 6
♦ A K 6 5 3 2
♣ –

SOUTH
♠ A K 10 9 8 4
♥ 10 5
♦ 7
♣ A K 6 5

A quick calculation of the high card points held by the two partnerships will show that North-South hold 26 high card points (North 12, South 14) and four length points (2 in each hand). East-West hold 14 high card points (of which East has 11) and five length points (East 3, West 2). Twenty-six high card points should have made North-South look for game and stop there, and a point-watching East-West should have said Pass throughout the auction. In the event, the bidding was:

NORTH	EAST	SOUTH	WEST
	1 ♦	2 ♠	5 ♦
5 ♠	6 ♦	6 ♠	PASS
PASS	PASS		

East's opening bid of One Diamond may at first sight be construed as a little adventurous but was eminently correct because she wanted to tell her partner about her diamonds, which were spectacularly good, even though she only had 11 high card points and three length points. And she was right to do so. South, holding a very strong hand bid Two Spades because he had six spades and 14 high card points. Overcalling, (that is, bidding after an opponent has opened the bidding) is usually only advisable when you have a five card suit or longer, although a point count of no more than 10 high card points is enough to make an overcall at the one level. With 14 high card points and a six card suit, there is no need to pussyfoot around at the one level. Jump to Two Spades and tell your partner what you hold.

Now it was West's turn to speak. To reach game in a minor suit like diamonds, the partnership ought to have something like 28 or 29 high card points, but West intended his Five Diamond bid as a sacrifice (see glossary).

North had something to offer and at this point he chucked his hat into the ring with a bid of Five Spades. This was music to South's ears, and confirmed that East-West had diamonds and North-South had a fit in spades. Under those circumstances, spades will usually triumph, because they rank higher on the bidding ladder than diamonds. But East was not finished yet. She wanted to buy the contract, even if originally she had not been thinking along the lines of a slam. She tried Six Diamonds. South, with only one diamond and firm support from his partner, was not to be outdone and bid Six Spades, even though he knew that he did not have the points theoretically required for a small slam. There was a distinct element of gambling in the bid, but he succeeded in reaching a playable contract.

And what happened then? West led the queen of diamonds, the normal lead, which was ruffed in Dummy. A careful look at Dummy, and South was able to lay down the cards and claim twelve tricks, conceding a trick to the ace of hearts. East-West would perhaps have made eleven tricks in diamonds, but they always had two losing hearts which would have prevented them from making a slam. But with a mere 14 high card points between them, they still had enough trick-winning power to have made game in diamonds.

I have included this hand to illustrate an important bidding lesson: the point of this hand is that with distributed hands like the ones held here, you should keep bidding more than on balanced hands. 'So far so good' may be echoing in your ears, but I assure you the landing will probably be soft enough.

Is there anything that East-West could have done to have snatched triumph from disaster? Well yes, there is one crafty bid that might have saved them. East, instead of bidding Six Diamonds, could have bid Six Clubs. At first glance, it seems crazy to bid Six of the one suit you are void in, but by this stage East-West may have suspected that their minor suit was not going to buy the contract against North-South's major, so by bidding Six Clubs, East could at least have given West a hint about what suit to lead against the contract. East would have ruffed a club opening lead, and then her ace of hearts would have been enough to defeat the contract.

POINTS SCHMOINTS

The hand just discussed is a good example of Points Schmoints. In my early days in bridge, I used to play with a man called Ira Rubin. He was a New Yorker who was not a believer in sticking slavishly to the rules. 'Points Schmoints,' he used to say when I suggested that on the hand he held his high card points were insufficient to make the contract he bid. 'Only schmigeggies live by points. A human being feels the power of the cards.' I have never really been able to work out the definition of a schmigeggie, but I think I know what Ira meant. If for instance your opponents have bid a grand slam and you have three kings, nine points, wouldn't you prefer to have just one ace, even though it is theoretically worth only four points? Yes. Ira was right. High card points are a very good guide, but good judgment is more important. I have tried all my bridge life since then to avoid being classified as a schmigeggie, if only because it is so hard to spell, and I like to think that I do try to feel the power of the cards. Whether I can feel it as strongly as a lady I knew who said she was always turned on by a void, I cannot be sure, but I can certainly feel the power of that one ace against a grand slam bid far more strongly than the doubtful strength of the three kings.

CONVENTIONAL BIDS

Bidding is most comfortable when it is natural. If I bid clubs, that is because my best suit is clubs. If my partner bids spades, that means his best suit is spades. However, there are times when we need to get across to our partner some information about our hand which cannot be done by natural bidding. This is when we need to consider using a conventional bid. A convention is formally described as an artificial bid which, by agreement or understanding between partners, serves to convey a meaning other than would be attributed to it by the opponents in the absence of an explanation. In other words, when I make an opening bid of Two Clubs, I do not mean I want to play a contract to make eight tricks with clubs as trumps: what I am trying to do is to convey some additional information to my partner about my hand. This is called a convention.

The difficulty about this is that if my partner misunderstands my conventional bid, we could be making things more rather than less complicated for ourselves and could end up with a contract that neither of us wants to play. So my advice is to use as few conventional bids as possible. However, there are three conventions which are routinely used. They are called the Stayman Convention, the Blackwood Convention and the Two Club Opening. Let's take a look at them.

THE STAYMAN CONVENTION

The Stayman Convention is named after Sam Stayman, the New York bridge player who felt the need to be able to respond to a One No Trump opening bid in such a way as to locate an eight card major suit fit, if it existed.

If you were dealt this hand:

♠ K 7 3   ♥ A J 8 6   ♦ A Q 9 4   ♣ 3 2

you have 14 points and a balanced hand, exactly right for a One No Trump opening bid. Partner hears the bid and knows roughly what to expect.

But suppose Partner holds something like:

♠ A J 5   ♥ K Q 9 5   ♦ K J 10 8   ♣ J 5

how does he respond? Even though he has 15 high card points, giving a combined total easily enough to make game, you can see that No Trumps is a dangerous contract to be in as there could be at least five tricks lost if clubs are led. But if the contract was Four Hearts, then clubs would only yield two tricks to the defence, before the Declarer could start ruffing. How can partner find out about the compatibility of hearts in the two hands? A bid of Two Hearts would routinely be considered a sign of weakness, meaning, 'I haven't got much, let's stop here.' Three Hearts is meant to show at least a five card heart suit, which we do not have, and Four Hearts would imply a six card suit. Stayman invented the conventional response of Two Clubs, which does not mean, 'Let's play in clubs.' It asks specifically, 'Do you have a four card major suit?' (Look back to our second example hand on page 27 in this chapter and you will see that North did precisely this).

In this particular case, the Responder, the Opener's partner, has only two clubs, but that does not stop him from bidding Two Clubs. His partner, realising he has been asked for information about his major suits (spades and hearts) can say, Two Hearts, which tells Responder that he has a four card heart suit. Thus they have found the suit to play the contract in. If the Opener had not had a four card major, he would have bid Two Diamonds, which does not mean, 'Let's try diamonds.' It means, 'I do not have either four hearts or four spades.' In that case, because he would most likely have a reasonable holding in clubs (Responder's weakness), Responder would be happy to play in No Trumps, and with 15 high card points bid Three No Trumps for game. If the Opener bids the wrong major, in other words if Responder has four hearts and three spades, and the Opener bids Two Spades, Responder would revert to No Trumps, knowing that there was no major suit fit, and take his chances on the club suit.

Stayman may look complicated at first sight, but it is a straightforward convention used when a Responder to a One No Trump opening wants to find a fit for his four card major. Obviously, if Responder does not have a four card major, he does not use Stayman. As soon as you hear an opponent open One No Trump, listen for Stayman. If his partner responds Two Clubs, then Opener's next bid will tell you a lot about his hand. Two Diamonds – no four card major; Two Hearts – I've got four hearts in my hand; Two Spades – I've got four spades in my hand. The subsequent bid by Responder tells you even more. Two No Trumps – you haven't got the same major as me, and I'm not sure if we can make game. I'll leave it to you. Three No Trumps – you haven't got the same major as me, but I've a good hand which should make us game. If Responder raises Opener's suit, they have found their fit. The level of Responder's rebid tells you more about the strength of his hand. If he raises to the three level, he probably has 11 or 12 high card points, because it can be inferred that he is interested in game but does not have enough high card points to bid it himself. A bid at the four level, enough for game, says he holds at least 13 high card points, while if he passes he has a minimum hand.

THE BLACKWOOD CONVENTION

The Blackwood Convention was invented by Easley Blackwood of Indianapolis. It is used when you and your partner feel you have enough combined points for a slam, but want to make sure that you hold enough aces. If your opponents hold two aces, a slam will go down, and sometimes you might be bidding beyond game without realising when to stop. Blackwood is a method of checking the number of aces and kings that the partnership holds. It works as follows.

A member of the partnership that thinks it has enough combined points for a slam bids Four No Trumps. This bid is bridge bidding language for 'How many aces have you got partner?' The replies use the suit rankings from the bottom up and begin at the next possible level of bidding, ie, the five level. They are:

Five Clubs – 'I have no aces.' OR 'I have four aces,' although this second translation is rare.

Five Diamonds – 'I have one ace.'

Five Hearts – 'I have two aces.'

Five Spades – 'I have three aces.'

A subsequent bid of Five No Trumps is bridge bidding language for, 'How many kings have you got partner?' Similarly the replies are:

Six Clubs – 'I have no kings.' OR 'I have four kings,' but as with aces, this is rare.

Six Diamonds – 'I have one king.'

Six Hearts – 'I have two kings.'

Six Spades – 'I have three kings.'

Here is a hand from a recent tournament (see opposite), which shows how Blackwood is useful.

South opened the bidding:

NORTH	EAST	SOUTH	WEST
		1 ♠	PASS
2 ♦	PASS	2 ♥	PASS
3 ♠	PASS	4 ♠	PASS
4 NT	PASS	5 ♦	PASS
6 ♠	PASS	PASS	PASS

When North bid Four No Trumps he used the Blackwood Convention. He believed that he and his partner had enough points for a slam in spades (they actually had 33 high card points and 2 length points). By bidding Four No Trumps, North was asking his partner to tell him how many aces he held. Partner may not simply say, 'I've got one ace.' He must reply in the language of bridge. Partner said Five Diamonds, which means the same thing. Armed

HAND

5

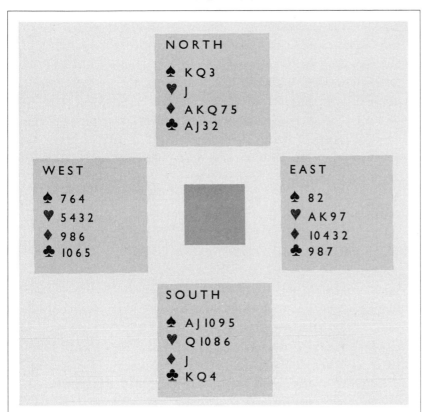

NORTH

♠ K Q 3
♥ J
♦ A K Q 7 5
♣ A J 3 2

WEST

♠ 7 6 4
♥ 5 4 3 2
♦ 9 8 6
♣ 1 0 6 5

EAST

♠ 8 2
♥ A K 9 7
♦ 1 0 4 3 2
♣ 9 8 7

SOUTH

♠ A J 1 0 9 5
♥ Q 1 0 8 6
♦ J
♣ K Q 4

with that information, North can go on comfortably to small slam. In this case, North bid Six Spades, and the contract ended successfully there.

Blackwood is very common when bidding for a slam, and a rather useful weapon to have in your arsenal.

THE TWO CLUB OPENING

The third important conventional bid is the Two Club Opening bid. This bid says nothing about clubs but does say you have at least 23 points in your hand, in high cards or length. It demands a response from your partner even if he has no points at all. It is therefore known as a forcing bid or a bid that insists that partner respond in order to keep the bidding open to game.

You might have been dealt:

♠ A 9   ♥ A K Q 10 9 8 6   ♦ A Q J 6   ♣ –

and despite your void in clubs, the correct opening bid with 20 high card points and three length points is Two

Clubs. Your partner must respond, and you can mention your hearts next time round. The advantage of the Two Club opening bid is that although an opening bid of Two Hearts suggests a good hand and would strongly *invite* partner to respond and perhaps lead to a game bid; an opening bid of Two Clubs *forces* partner to reply, because even if partner only has three high card points, the partnership is already in the game zone (23+3=26). So partner *must* reply and support where possible. However to show a bad hand a response of Two Diamonds is used as a negative.

BLUFF OR PSYCHIC BIDS

Psychic bids can be double-edged weapons. Trying to bluff your opponents in bidding is a dangerous pastime, because more often than not you bluff your partner as well. I would not advise the use of bluff bids. However, that is not to say they do not work from time to time.

I was playing in a World Championship match in Jamaica a couple of years ago.

My hand was a good one:

♠ A 10742   ♥ –   ♦ 85   ♣ A Q 10963

But I did the wrong thing. I was East. The bidding was:

WEST	NORTH	EAST	SOUTH
			4 ♥
PASS	4 NT	PASS	5 ♦
PASS	5 ♥	PASS	PASS
PASS			

I had to decide whether North's Four No Trump bid was a bluff. I looked at my opponent but he was completely inscrutable, not even blinking. How could I tell what to do? Well, here is my excuse for what followed. While I was trying to decide, a bee flew into the room, circled our bidding screen and swooped down and stung the Blackwood bidder on the cheek. He still did not blink. That was enough for me. Anybody who did not have enough high cards for that bid surely would have screamed, or at least reacted. I was convinced that only a genuinely big hand would have been enough to make him ignore the pain. I passed confidently despite my massive hand, and missed a slam. If only I had analysed the auction rather than rely on the effects of a bee sting, I would have seen that he must be bluffing. The response to his Blackwood bid was Five Diamonds, one ace, as many as he could reasonably expect from a pre-empt, yet he signed off below a slam. That is not the sign of a strong hand.

Here is the full hand:

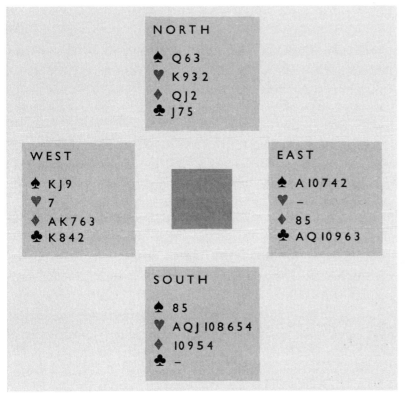

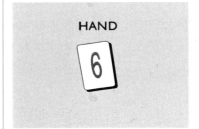

HAND
6

I should have used my brain to recognise the bluff and not relied on the power of the venom of a bee!

As an experiment I gave the hand to my pupils, with the same bidding by North-South. They made short work of it:

WEST	NORTH	EAST	SOUTH
			4 ♥
PASS	4 NT	5 ♣	PASS
6 ♣	PASS	PASS	PASS

East bid far more aggressively than I had done, yet he was not really risking disaster. Once North had bid Four

No Trumps, East had to make a decision. He rightly chose to bid, following the rule of bidding up on a distributional hand. South no longer had to bid and now passed. West took the reasonable risk of raising the contract to Six Clubs, and in the event the defence only made one heart trick, and the Six Club contract was made. The lesson is that there is nobody in the world who does not make mistakes, and beginners can do as well as experts.

RULES OF COMPETITIVE BIDDING

However, it pays to remember the golden rules of competitive bidding, which I had forgotten in the World Championships. Here they are:

1 The most important rule is the rule of overcalling. What you must have is a good suit; this is more important than high card points alone. Overcall only with good *texture* and *length* in your suits. *Defend* with balanced hands.

2 In a competitive auction, bridge is a bidder's game. With unbalanced or distributional hands, fortune favours the brave, so pluck up your courage and bid.

3 When the opponents stop comfortably at the two level (the partscore zone) having found a fit, make life uncomfortable for them and bid or double (a bid used to increase the size of the penalty if the opponents' contract fails. It shows that you have little faith in the opponents' ability to make their contract). By bidding you may push them up to the dangers of the three level. *Remember* it is safer to do this when the opponents have announced a fit, ie, One Heart, Pass, Two Hearts, Pass, not a potential *misfit*, ie, One Heart, One No Trump, Two Diamonds, Pass.

PARTNERSHIP HARMONY

Bridge is a partnership game, and it is as important to remember that as it is to bid the right contract. Bidding is not always a precise language, because with fewer than two dozen words, you have to convey a massive range of possibilities and desires, and we are all human and very fallible. But it is up to both partners to take mishaps in their stride and play the next hand amicably, even if the last was a disaster.

I watched my pupils play the following hand:

HAND

7

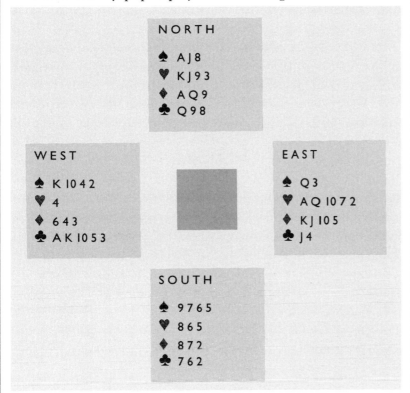

NORTH
♠ A J 8
♥ K J 9 3
♦ A Q 9
♣ Q 9 8

WEST
♠ K 10 4 2
♥ 4
♦ 6 4 3
♣ A K 10 5 3

EAST
♠ Q 3
♥ A Q 10 7 2
♦ K J 10 5
♣ J 4

SOUTH
♠ 9 7 6 5
♥ 8 6 5
♦ 8 7 2
♣ 7 6 2

The bidding went like this:

SOUTH	WEST	NORTH	EAST
			1 ♥
PASS	2 ♣	DOUBLE	PASS
2 ♠	DOUBLE	PASS	PASS
PASS	PASS		

A takeout double, North's bid, in bridge bidding language, says to partner, 'Bid a suit. I have a good hand with the unbid suits. Show me which one you prefer.' Your partner should respond. In this case South bid Two Spades which was doubled. North-South went down, not surprisingly in view of their combined holding of 17 high card points *and* all concentrated in North. South was most upset at having found himself in Two Spades Doubled. He felt this was the result of North's unnecessary double of the Two Club bid and told North just what he thought of her double. North felt that her double was justified, after all with 17 points, she felt obliged to enter the bidding.

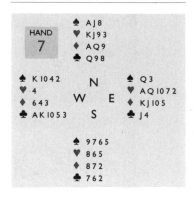

HAND
7

♠ A J 8
♥ K J 9 3
♦ A Q 9
♣ Q 9 8

♠ K 10 4 2
♥ 4
♦ 6 4 3
♣ A K 10 5 3

♠ Q 3
♥ A Q 10 7 2
♦ K J 10 5
♣ J 4

N
W   E
S

♠ 9 7 6 5
♥ 8 6 5
♦ 8 7 2
♣ 7 6 2

What else could she do but invite partner to pick an unbid suit? How could she know he had no points at all?

Who was right?

Actually South was right about the bidding, but wrong in his reaction. It is very important, although sometimes difficult, to be gentle on your partner at such times. It is at precisely these moments that we need to control our emotions. Bridge is a social game, not a prelude to World War Three. Perhaps North should have passed rather than doubled. Perhaps North-South were unlucky that East-West did not help them out and try for a contract rather than being content to defend, but whatever the rights and wrongs, the fact is that we are all very prone to error and there will be times when you find yourself playing an impossible, even a ridiculous, contract. When that happens, just chalk it up to experience. Playing, playing and playing again is the only way to improve. Fighting won't help.

DECLARER PLAY

You have bought the contract at the auction, and you are Declarer. What bliss! Declarer play is the part of bridge which is closest to everybody's heart. You play your own hand and the Dummy. As with any part of bridge, you will not become an expert with just one or two lessons, you have to play and play again. Although you know you will get an opportunity to practise your bidding technique with every hand that is dealt, you will only have a chance to be Declarer, by the law of averages, on one hand in four. Seize the opportunity, and by the standard of your play make your partners want you to become Declarer whenever possible. That way you might defeat the law of averages, and play the Dummy more often than one hand in four.

But first do you ever find that when the lead is made and Dummy comes down, your mind goes blank? It's not unusual. The most common problem with beginners as Declarer is what I call the Blob Syndrome. As your left hand opponent makes the opening lead, and Dummy lays down his hand, your mind becomes a big blob with no clear line of thought. The Blob Syndrome player tries a little bit of this, then a little bit of that; but, with no clear route to his goal, he usually does not reach it. My purpose is to banish the blob from your mind and replace it with an ordered method of improving your Declarer play. There are several points to concentrate on to improve your Declarer play. Here are some of them.

HANDLING YOUR TRUMPS

The first thing you learn when you play in a suit contract is that you have a secret weapon called the trump suit.

Even the smallest card in that suit can win a trick from a mighty ace. It is, however, a secret weapon that is often mishandled by beginners. As soon as they learn that they can use this weapon, they start ruffing (winning tricks with trumps) everything in sight, rather like a child thrashing around in the bathtub. Handling trumps is a delicate subject requiring direction and care.

Beginners are taught to draw trumps (play trumps out to make sure that the opponents have none left to ruff with) as soon as possible, and generally that is a sensible course of action. But it is not always the best plan. Sometimes you need those trumps.

Take a look at this hand:

HAND 8

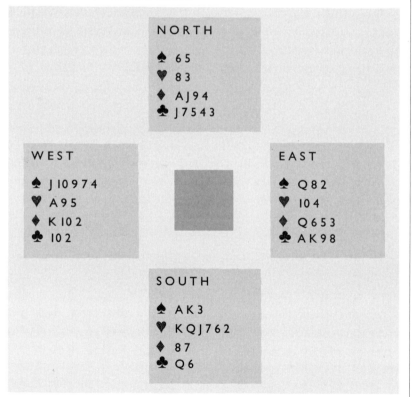

NORTH
♠ 6 5
♥ 8 3
♦ A J 9 4
♣ J 7 5 4 3

WEST
♠ J 10 9 7 4
♥ A 9 5
♦ K 10 2
♣ 10 2

EAST
♠ Q 8 2
♥ 10 4
♦ Q 6 5 3
♣ A K 9 8

SOUTH
♠ A K 3
♥ K Q J 7 6 2
♦ 8 7
♣ Q 6

Bidding:

NORTH	EAST	SOUTH	WEST
	PASS	1 ♥	PASS
1 NT	PASS	3 ♥	PASS
PASS	PASS		

South overbid a little, landing in a contract of Three

Hearts. West led the jack of spades, which South wins in his hand. With one trick under his belt and the lead in his hand, the first reaction with six trumps might be to draw trumps. But wait a minute. South needs to make nine tricks, and unless he gets rid of that little losing spade in his hand, the contract will fail. So he needs to play two more rounds of spades, ruffing the three of spades in Dummy on the second round, in order to turn it into a winner. When South plays trumps, West may win his ace and play a fourth spade and East may put his ten of hearts on. If South overruffs he goes down, but if he simply throws away clubs all will be well.

In America, they sometimes refer to drawing trumps as 'getting the kiddies off the street.' In Pakistan, we talk about pulling your opponents' teeth out. The American expression refers to playing safe and the Pakistani expression to removing your opponents' strength. Both are warnings about the perils of Declarer not drawing trumps. However as the hand above showed, it is not always wise to draw trumps instantly. It is wiser to strike a balance between getting rid of your losers and drawing trumps.

THE STOP PROCEDURE

Perhaps the most useful guide I know to good Declarer play is what I call the STOP procedure. I can promise you that if you apply STOP to every hand you play, you will greatly improve your success rate.

The letters of the word STOP stand for the four fundamental steps you need to go through on each and every hand.

S – STOP to consider your goal
T – TALLY your winners and losers
O – ORGANISE your plan
P – PUT your plan into action.

That looks easy enough, but what does STOP really mean? First of all, let us consider the first step:

STOP to consider your goal. The most important of those words is the first, stop. Pause for a moment. When the Dummy is on the table, there is no law that says you must rush headlong into playing the first card you see. Stop, and consider your goal. Your goal is easy to define. It is whatever your contract says it should be. If the contract is Two No Trumps, your goal is to win eight tricks with no suit as trumps. If the contract is Seven Spades, then your goal is to win all the tricks, with spades as trumps. The reason I stress this is twofold:

1 it always pays to think before you touch a card from Dummy, no matter how easy the hand looks, and

2 when you remind yourself of your goal, you avoid the common error of making unnecessary plays that may give you overtricks, but that may also put your contract at risk.

TALLY your winners and losers. How do you tally your winners and losers? It is easy enough. Once you have decided what your goal is, you need to understand how near you are to getting there. If your contract is One No Trump, and you control all four aces and all four kings, you have eight sure tricks, and that is enough for your contract. (If you had all those top cards between you and the bidding stopped at One No Trump, you need to go back to the last chapter to sharpen up your bidding skills, but that is beside the point). As a general rule, if you are playing in No Trumps, you need to count how many winners you have. There is nothing complicated about counting winners: they are cards which will certainly win the trick when played. If you are playing a suit contract, then count the number of losers you have, and look at ways of ruffing or discarding those losers.

You also need to be careful in your definition of a winner. For example, if the contract is in No Trumps and Dummy holds ♠ A K 7 and you hold ♠ Q 4 2, there are three sure tricks here, the ace, king and queen of spades. If Dummy held ♠ K 10 7 and you held ♠ Q 4 2, there would be no sure tricks in this suit. If you can drive out the ace successfully, then you may have one or two winners, but you cannot do that without giving up the lead once. So there are no quick winners there. If Dummy holds ♠ A J and Declarer holds ♠ K Q, there are still only two sure tricks here, because although the top four spades are there, they will be used up after two rounds of spades. Two honours on each trick. There can be no more winners in any suit than there are cards in the hand.

Let us consider this complete pair of hands:

Dummy – ♠ A 7 4   ♥ Q J   ♦ Q 6 5 3   ♣ A Q 6 2

Declarer – ♠ K 9 6   ♥ A K   ♦ A K 9 7 4 2   ♣ 9 7

In a No Trump contract, we have two spade winners, two heart winners, six diamond winners and one club winner, a total of 11 winners. If our contract is Five No Trumps, we do not have to look any further. If we need to look for more than 11 tricks, we will have to consider either promoting cards to become winners, or as in this case finessing (trying to win a trick with a high card when you know a higher card is held by your opponents, but you don't know which opponent holds the higher card) to create winners. The obvious suit to try to promote a winner in is clubs, where the queen may be a winner if we finesse (see page 49) and the king is well placed, ie, before the ace and the queen in Dummy.

One final thought as we tally out winners and losers: if after your tally, it looks as if the contract is easy, be pessimistic. Think what could go wrong and look out for the dangers that might be lurking unexpectedly in the seemingly easy hands. If after your tally, things look terrible, be optimistic. Search out the silver linings in difficult hands. Now think positively and hope that every card lies well. If you play all your easy hands on the carefree basis that even a palooka (a very bad bridge player) could make this contract, you could subsequently find yourself in trouble and a good contract could be thrown away. If you look optimistically on what you have been given to play with, who knows, some of your more outlandish ideas might work, and you might yet scrape home.

<u>ORGANISE your plan.</u> Using the same hand: If a club has been led, and our contract is Five Diamonds, we need only 11 tricks. So obviously we play the ace of clubs to win the trick, and then we hasten to draw trumps. We have 11 sure tricks (2 spades, 2 hearts, 6 diamonds and 1 club), so we must not put any of them in jeopardy by looking for a complicated way to make an overtrick. Organisation can take much longer than this if the contract is a difficult one,

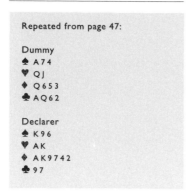

Repeated from page 47:

Dummy
♠ A74
♥ QJ
♦ Q653
♣ AQ62

Declarer
♠ K96
♥ AK
♦ AK9742
♣ 97

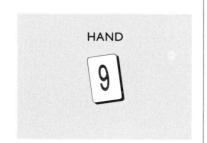

HAND

9

but the principle remains: work out what you are going to do, and then do it. It is far easier to work out how to play a hand before any tricks have been won or lost than to try to re-organise yourself halfway through the play, when you cannot quite remember who had which card, how many hearts Dummy started with, and whether East threw a spade or a club on the fourth diamond trick. If you are not organised before you start playing for the contract, you have no chance of organising yourself once it has started slipping away.

<u>PUT your plan into action.</u> Here play the ace, draw trumps and run through your winners until the contract is made. Then you may find that the way the cards have fallen has allowed you to make an extra trick or two, or you may find that you just make the contract. Whatever happens, you have done what you set out to achieve, and you have not put the contract at risk by being tempted by the lure of an unnecessary play.

Here is a hand which I used as an exercise for my pupils:

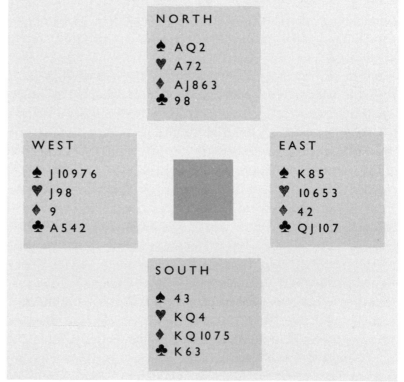

NORTH
♠ AQ2
♥ A72
♦ AJ863
♣ 98

WEST
♠ J10976
♥ J98
♦ 9
♣ A542

EAST
♠ K85
♥ 10653
♦ 42
♣ QJ107

SOUTH
♠ 43
♥ KQ4
♦ KQ1075
♣ K63

The contract was Three No Trumps, which for a

partnership with 28 high card points between them, ought to be rather easy. In practice Declarer took one look at the hand, after the lead of the jack of spades from West, and then straight away took the spade finesse. Unluckily for him, not only did it not work, but East switched to the queen of clubs and continued the suit. Eventually the defence made four club tricks and one spade trick and the contract went down. This sort of mistake is common enough. Declarer sees a tempting opportunity for a finesse, but it is pointless to finesse when there is no need.

Let us think how the STOP procedure would have helped us in this case. The contract is Three No Trumps, a game contract, and the jack of spades has been led by West. Before we touch a card we STOP. Step one tells us to stop to consider our goal. Well, in this case our goal is to take nine tricks with no suit as trumps. That means we cannot afford to lose more than four tricks. However, a TALLY of the winners in Declarer and Dummy shows us we already have the nine tricks we need – the ace of spades, ace king and queen of hearts, and the five diamond honours. So when we think about how to ORGANISE our plan, the only thing to avoid is a risky finesse or playing on clubs. The hand is fairly straightforward if we play it straightforwardly. To PUT our plan into action is easy. Win the first trick with the ace of spades, and then run the hearts and diamonds until we take our nine tricks. The STOP procedure is designed to make things simple, and while that may mean from time to time you cut out the flashy plays that might impress your partner but are not necessary, you will be even more impressive by your consistent winning play.

THE FINESSE

My dictionary defines finesse as 'elegant skill in style or performance' and for many beginners a finesse retains that meaning in bridge. It also means an attempt to take a trick with a card when opponents hold a higher card, but the successful finesse is, of course, elegant skill in style or performance, which we all love to bring off from time to time. The temptation of a finesse is so great that beginners long to try it. But experts would rather think of it as an apple in the Garden of Eden. It is very tempting but it should only be used as a last resort, because you often find that it is followed by a sudden fall. Like all fruit, tempting apples can be eaten at the end of the meal, so postpone your finesse to the very end if possible. Then, as we have seen, it may not be needed.

Let us assume you hold ♥ 7 3 2 and Dummy holds ♥ K 6 5. You do not know where the ace is, but until it is played, you cannot count the king in Dummy as a winner. If you lead a low heart from Declarer's hand, towards the king in Dummy you will make a trick whenever West has the ace. A 50-50 chance. If East has the ace and wins, then the finesse did not work. But there was at least a 50% chance of success, which is better than nothing if a contract depends on it. But it is worse than nothing if the contract does not depend on it. Risking the success of a contract just for a piece of elegant skill is irresponsible. It is not the kind of play that will impress your partner.

The point of a finesse is to win a trick with a card when your opponents hold a higher card in that suit: it gives you a trick which you would not otherwise have won. If the finesse could either lose you a sure trick or not make any more tricks than you safely have, then you should not attempt it.

Take a look at the hand shown on the next page, which is an example of an expert resisting the temptation to finesse until the last possible moment.

The bidding went like this:

NORTH	EAST	SOUTH	WEST
	PASS	1 ♣	PASS
1 ♦	PASS	2 NT	PASS
6 NT	PASS	PASS	PASS

The two of diamonds is led by West. A quick look at Dummy shows that North-South are in a good contract. But remember that seemingly easy hands can be deceptive. Declarer's first reaction might be immediately to start taking one of the available finesses; but this could be a mistake until he has put his STOP procedure into action.

If Declarer STOPs, then a proper plan of attack

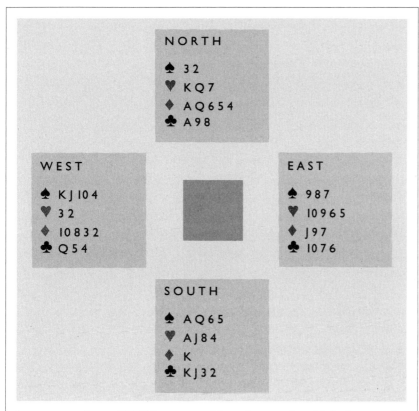

NORTH
- ♠ 3 2
- ♥ K Q 7
- ♦ A Q 6 5 4
- ♣ A 9 8

WEST
- ♠ K J 10 4
- ♥ 3 2
- ♦ 10 8 3 2
- ♣ Q 5 4

EAST
- ♠ 9 8 7
- ♥ 10 9 6 5
- ♦ J 9 7
- ♣ 10 7 6

SOUTH
- ♠ A Q 6 5
- ♥ A J 8 4
- ♦ K
- ♣ K J 3 2

becomes clear. STOP to consider the goal, which is to take twelve tricks in No Trumps. Not an easy one, this, but the contract is there to be made. A TALLY of winners shows there are ten (one spade, four hearts, three diamonds and two clubs) so two more have to be found. If you ORGANISE the plan around the club finesse, and if it works and the clubs split the contract will make because with four club tricks, the total of winners is boosted by two, to 12. However to PUT that plan into operation is rather risky, because Declarer would be relying on luck. Perhaps it could be played better. Let me tell you what I would do.

I STOP and make a TALLY. I realise I have ten top tricks. It looks as though I should ORGANISE my play around a finesse, but I like to get as far into the contract as possible before having to resort to finessing. I can promote an extra trick in diamonds if the suit is divided four and three. So I PUT my plan into action and begin by winning the diamond in my hand. Then I cash three rounds of hearts, ending up in Dummy. After that come my two diamond winners in Dummy, discarding two spades from

HAND

my hand. At this stage, after six tricks, I know I can create an extra trick from diamonds by giving up a trick. At this stage the cards looked like this:

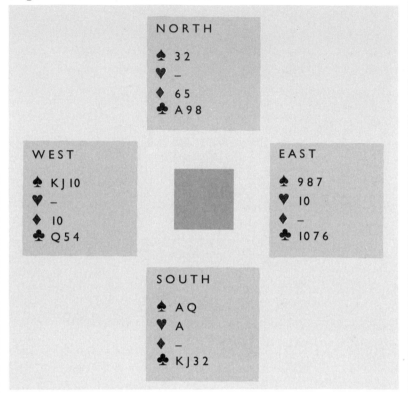

NORTH
♠ 3 2
♥ –
♦ 6 5
♣ A 9 8

WEST
♠ K J 10
♥ –
♦ 10
♣ Q 5 4

EAST
♠ 9 8 7
♥ 10
♦ –
♣ 10 7 6

SOUTH
♠ A Q
♥ A
♦ –
♣ K J 3 2

I had still not taken any finesse, but I was on target to make the contract. My next move is to play another diamond from Dummy. I lead the six, East discards a spade and I discard a club from my hand. West wins the trick with his 10, but then is faced with the prospect of leading into either my spades or my clubs. Whichever suit he chooses, I am creating an extra trick without having to finesse. If he leads a low club, although I do not know for sure where the queen of clubs is, I am bound to make an extra club trick. If he leads a spade, both my queen and my ace become winners whoever holds the king. And of course, my last diamond in Dummy is a winner too. That gives me the contract, without having to finesse at all.

The point of this example is to remind you to STOP before you begin to play the contract. Waiting may well make depending on luck unnecessary, and one of the key elements of good Declarer play is the art of swinging the odds in your favour.

DUCKING

One of the great charms of bridge is that we use such descriptive language. Take the word ducking, for instance. It just means that you deliberately lose a trick you could have won, or tried to win, opting out of the main action, so to speak, until you are ready. Used correctly it is a very useful technique.

Look at this hand:

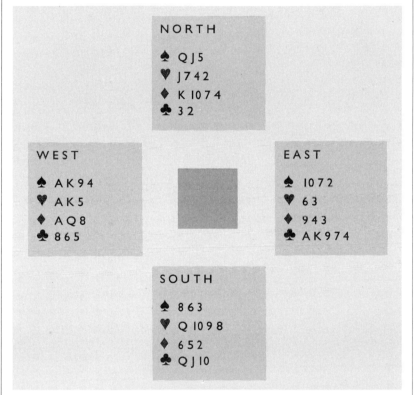

NORTH
♠ Q J 5
♥ J 7 4 2
♦ K 10 7 4
♣ 3 2

WEST
♠ A K 9 4
♥ A K 5
♦ A Q 8
♣ 8 6 5

EAST
♠ 10 7 2
♥ 6 3
♦ 9 4 3
♣ A K 9 7 4

SOUTH
♠ 8 6 3
♥ Q 10 9 8
♦ 6 5 2
♣ Q J 10

Declarer (West) has contracted to make Three No Trumps. North has led the two of hearts. Declarer goes into the STOP procedure. His goal is to take nine tricks, and when he tallies his winners, he finds that can make five tricks in his hand and two more in Dummy. That makes seven, but he needs to find two more from somewhere. Clubs look like the most probable source of winners, but Dummy's small clubs will not be promoted to winners until at least three rounds of clubs have been played, assuming there is a three-two split of clubs. However, if Declarer wins the first club trick with his ace in Dummy, and then plays his king, followed by a small

```
        ♠ Q J 5
HAND    ♥ J 7 4 2
 12     ♦ K 10 7 4
        ♣ 3 2

♠ A K 9 4      N       ♠ 10 7 2
♥ A K 5              ♥ 6 3
♦ A Q 8    W     E    ♦ 9 4 3
♣ 8 6 5        S      ♣ A K 9 7 4

        ♠ 8 6 3
        ♥ Q 10 9 8
        ♦ 6 5 2
        ♣ Q J 10
```

club, his two other clubs will be useless because he will not be able to get back to them. He has no other entry in Dummy, so cannot get there to cash his clubs when everybody else is out of them. He will have made his two original winners in clubs but no more. However, by ducking the first round of clubs, ie, by playing a small club from Dummy so that South wins the first club trick with one of his honours, Declarer will later win the lead back and can play to his clubs in Dummy. He will now win four tricks in clubs, and make his contract. This ducking play is standard procedure and occurs often.

THE ODDS

It would be wrong to make you feel that bridge was a complicated mathematical game, but all the same it helps if you have some idea of the odds of a particular play working before you attempt it. People have worked out the odds of every conceivable deal, and of the likely distribution of cards among the defence. You do not need to know, for example, that there is a 30% chance you will have no aces in any hand you receive, which means that of every 10 hands you are dealt, three will contain no aces. It is not particularly encouraging to know, as you sort your cards and discover no card higher than a nine in any suit, that your yarborough was a 1827 to 1 against longshot before it found its way into your hand. However, it is useful to know that 47.3% of hands dealt are balanced hands, but there is only a 1 in 25 chance of a seven card or longer suit.

Even more important to know is the likely distribution of cards in a particular suit among your opponents. If you are Declarer and you hold seven cards in one suit between your hand and Dummy, how are the remaining six likely to be divided? Is it most likely that East has three and West has three? Surprisingly, the answer is no. The most likely distribution, mathematically speaking, is that one opponent has four and the other has two. That simple fact affects your play, as Declarer or Defender, when you are trying to place particular cards. Counting the cards is obviously very necessary for skilled Declarer play, but it is not really complicated. It is not a matter of having to remember every one of 52 cards as they are played. It is like typing. I have been trying to learn to type recently, and found it very difficult at first to remember where the keys were. But after a while it becomes second nature. I work by remembering hand patterns, by building up a mental picture of the hands by suits rather than by individual cards.

Without going into the full actuarial statistics, all you need to know at this stage is that if there are an odd number of cards held by the Defenders, then the most likely distribution is the most even break possible. In other words, if you hold eight cards and the defence has five, in the absence of any other evidence such as what was said at the auction, or what suit is led, it is most probable that one Defender has three and the other two, rather than a four-one split, or a five-nothing split. If you have six cards and the defence seven, the split will most likely be four-three rather than five-two, six-one or seven-void. If you have all but three cards in a suit, there are three chances in four that the split is two-one rather than three-zero, and if you are trying to account for nine cards in a suit, there is a better than evens chance that they split five-four, while there is only about a 12 to 1 chance that one hand holds seven cards and the other two.

But if you hold nine cards in a suit, and there are four held by the defence, the most likely split is the uneven three-one rather than the even two-two. There is an evens chance of the three-one split, but only a three in eight chance of the two-two split. The three-three split is rarer than four-two, and the four-four split occurs less often than five-three. An even number of cards will split rather oddly, and an uneven number will split fairly evenly.

INCREASING THE ODDS

In bridge as in life, it pays to increase the odds. A friend of mine, an American banker, likes to produce a dollar bill from his wallet and ask people to bet on whether the final digit of its serial number is odd or even. At first glance, it would appear you have a 50-50 chance whichever you say, but he points out that if you think back to when the first dollar bill was printed, that had the serial number

HAND

one, an odd number. Therefore, even if the most recently printed one has an even final digit, there is still no less than a 50-50 chance of an odd final digit, and if the most recently printed dollar bill has an odd final digit, then there is one more odd than even numbered dollar bill in circulation. So the odds are infinitesimally greater that any particular dollar bill will have an odd final digit, and therefore it is worth betting on the odd number, just to keep the odds fractionally in your favour. This competitive advantage may be so small as to be practically invisible, but the first principle of Declarer play, as in life, is to take whatever edge you can.

Here we have an example of getting the best out of a hand by giving yourself the best chance. A complicated example of expert thinking.

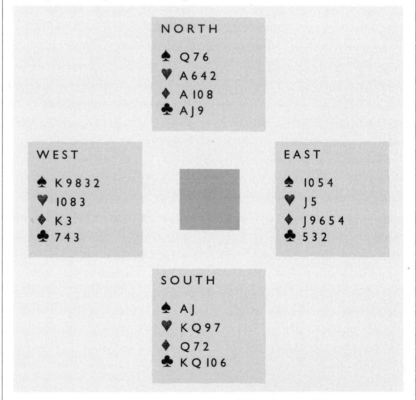

The contract is Six Hearts, and Declarer (South) STOPs to assess her chances on the lead of a small trump. The goal is 12 tricks, but the tally shows only nine winners. However, if the trumps break evenly, then the chances look much better: there would be 11 tricks. The obvious plan is to get the kiddies off the street and then to try the spade finesse for the twelfth trick. If the finesse works, the contract will make. So Declarer plays three rounds of trumps and then a small spade from Dummy reasoning that as she is always going to lose one diamond trick, if East has the king of spades, all will be well. Unfortunately, West holds the king of spades, the finesse fails and the contract goes down. Okay? Not okay.

There is another way of looking at this hand. At the outset, it certainly seems as though the only way to make the contract is by taking the spade finesse, but remember, the forbidden fruit should always be left to the end. Anything played before then that does not hinder the making of the contract can only be a help. My plan would be to draw trumps, then play four rounds of clubs, discarding a small diamond from Dummy on the fourth. There may be no real master plan. At this stage I am simply going through the motions. Then I would play the two of diamonds towards the ace in Dummy, followed by the last diamond from Dummy towards my queen. I am still intending to take the inevitable spade finesse later. West wins this trick with his king, but unknown to me at that time after nine tricks, with four left to play, the position is actually this, see page 58.

the position is actually this, see page 58.

West has the lead, and with only spades left is forced to play a spade into my ace jack, giving me my twelfth trick. The contract is made.

It's true I perhaps stumbled into the winning line as West started with only two diamonds and I was able to make the contract without a finesse, but by postponing the moment of truth for as long as possible and not committing myself to an early finesse I increased the odds slightly in my favour. Yes I was lucky, but I gave myself a chance to be lucky.

FINDING THE QUEEN AND SEXY PLAYS

I suppose it's something in my character, but I love flamboyant plays. I find the unexpected exhilarating. A good play which works, like the one I have just described, I call a sexy play. One that fails, as a result of mismanagement, is not so sexy. A sexy play is the result of a concept, a thought process that makes a winning play.

HAND

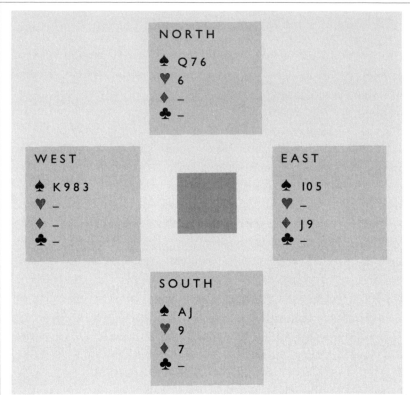

NORTH
♠ Q 7 6
♥ 6
♦ —
♣ —

WEST
♠ K 9 8 3
♥ —
♦ —
♣ —

EAST
♠ 10 5
♥ —
♦ J 9
♣ —

SOUTH
♠ A J
♥ 9
♦ 7
♣ —

When you are in a hopeless situation, it sometimes pays to do something strange, on the offchance that it will work. You have to do what you can to turn a desperate state of affairs into a victory. The line between genius and madness is, they say, a fine one, and the line between sexy and not so sexy plays can be equally indistinct. However if you play attacking bridge, if you try to get the defence before they get you, and follow the STOP procedure, you will come up with sexy plays more often than not.

One of the plays classified as sexy is the way a good Declarer always finds a missing queen. Bridge players are supposed to need to have a prodigious memory to be able to remember where all the key cards are being held, but in truth, there is no special magic involved. Often when there is a missing queen, you can usually work out where it is by following the available clues.

If Dummy holds ♥ A 10 5 4 and Declarer holds ♥ K J 9 7, the only thing preventing four heart tricks is the queen. Where is it? You might be tempted to try an immediate finesse. But wait. First of all, study any clues from the bidding. Was there perhaps a pre-emptive bid? If there was, the pre-emptor's partner would be the more likely holder of the missing queen, so finesse that way.

What is the distribution of the remaining hearts? With five cards, a suit usually breaks three-two, so if you find out who has three you should finesse him for the queen.

Then, of course, there is one of the bridge player's ten commandments which says, 'cover an honour with an honour,' (see page 67). If you lead the jack from your hand, quite often an unsuspecting opponent will cover when he has the queen. If he does not cover it is often because he cannot, ie, he does not have the queen, and so you could finesse the other way.

THE LAST TRUMP

Another piece of advice I would give if you find yourself in a desperate situation, is play the last trump. Many beginners are reluctant to part with their final trump because they see it as their security blanket. They never quite know when they are going to need it and frequently play off all their trumps except the last, hoping to squeeze their opponents. Usually nothing happens. But squeezes do work, even for those who are not technically very advanced. So if you are in a desperate situation and can see no chance of success, try playing off all your trumps. Who knows, maybe the last one will do the damage you are hoping for.

A FINAL WORD ON DECLARER PLAY

Declarer play is for me the most exciting part of this game, and it probably is for you. There is no guarantee that by following all the guidelines I have set out, you will make every contract you play. But if you follow the STOP procedure you will be successful more often than not.

DEFENCE

If the auction is the most intricate part of bridge, and Declarer play the most exciting, there is no doubt at all that defence is the most difficult. Defence is to bridge what brain surgery is to medicine. Or perhaps the Defender is to bridge what the saboteur is to war. The Defender is working in enemy territory (Declarer's contract), trying to bring about his defeat, but although he knows he has support from his own side, communications are difficult, his weapons are of doubtful strength and he finds himself exposed and out on his own more often than he would wish. Yet playing as part of the defence is something that happens on average every other hand, twice as often as being Declarer or sitting there helplessly as Dummy, so it is the part of the game where a sharpening of skills can bring immediate rewards.

Defence is a partnership, just like the auction and Declarer play, but the problems are great. By definition, the Defenders have not won the auction, so more often than not they have not told each other a great deal about their hands. All they know is that probably their combined strength is less than Declarer's, and in a suit contract they will almost certainly have fewer trumps. They also have the major disadvantage that they cannot see each other's hands during the playing of the contract. Declarer sees Dummy as soon as the opening lead has been made, and plans his strategy accordingly, but the Defenders cannot see what their partner holds, and therefore cannot be sure of their combined strengths and weaknesses.

The first thing the Defenders must do, therefore, even before thinking about the opening lead, is to STOP like Declarer, and work out a plan of sabotage. Just as Declarer needs a plan to make his contract, so the Defenders need a plan to defeat it. Unfortunately, they have to make their plans individually, and unless they can find ways of telling each other what they hold the danger is more of blowing up their own bridges, so to speak, than of planting their bombs in the right place to destroy Declarer's chances of ultimate victory. So communication between the Defenders needs to continue throughout the play, but not before each Defender has worked out what the objective of his sabotage is to be.

STOP.

As soon as the auction is over, whether it is you or your partner to lead, you must work out what you are trying to do.

Say, for example, that you hold this hand:

♠ Q J 10 9 2 ♥ 4 2 ♦ A 5 3 ♣ Q 10 2

A balanced hand with nine points. The contract is Three No Trumps, the opposition having bid One Club, One Diamond, One No Trump and finally Three No Trumps. You will have to make the opening lead, because your right hand opponent is Declarer. You STOP to consider your goal, which is to take at least five tricks to defeat the contract, with no suit as trumps. Simple enough, but the next question is to ask what weapons you hold to undertake some successful sabotage. TALLY your winners.

You have the ace of diamonds, so that is one winner. What else is a sure trick there? Nothing, at least not yet. You have only one winner, yet between your partner and yourself, you have to find four more to defeat the contract. The best area for you to develop winners is obviously your spades, where after the ace and king have gone, you could hold as many as three winners. That seems to be the important message you must get across to your partner. Neither you nor your partner bid in the auction, so you have little idea about the areas of strength in your partner's hand, but it is obviously right to ORGANISE your plan around turning your spades into winners.

PUT your plan into operation. Choose an opening lead and begin the defence. The logical and natural lead would be the top of a sequence in your best suit, in this case the queen of spades (see section on opening leads). As soon as that is led, you have some more information, because Dummy comes down, and you find out much more about what is likely to happen.

In this case, Dummy is:

♠ 7 6 5   ♥ K J 9   ♦ K J 9 8 7   ♣ K 4

Dummy has 11 high card points, a balanced hand. If you have nine points and Dummy 11, that leaves 20 for the other two hands. Declarer began with a bid of One Club, and given that he seems to have a balanced hand he should have 13 or more high card points, which leaves very few for your partner. If your partner has no more than a handful of points, there is little point on planning a defence around promoting winners in his hand. They are unlikely to be there.

Dummy plays the five of spades (with three little spades it does not make any difference which spade is played, of course) and it's partner's turn to STOP and think.

Here is partner's hand:

♠ K 3   ♥ 8 7 6 5 3   ♦ 4 2   ♣ 9 6 5 3

His thoughts may be along these lines: 'I have only three high card points: the king of spades. All in all not much of a hand to put to the cause of the defence. But the best thing about this hand is that my only honour is in the suit my partner has led, which is a hopeful sign. Should I play my three of spades on this trick or my king? Let's work it out. If Declarer has something like the ace and two small spades, which is likely, and I play my three, he will duck. On the play of the next spade, Declarer will duck again and I will be stuck in my hand with no more spades to play. ['Getting stuck' like this is called blocking.] Partner is likely to have the queen, jack and ten judging by his lead, so it must be better to overtake partner's lead with my king on the first trick, thus establishing our spade suit once the ace has gone. As soon as partner regains the lead he can cash his remaining spades.'

The complete hand is shown opposite.

That is how you will win five tricks (four in spades and

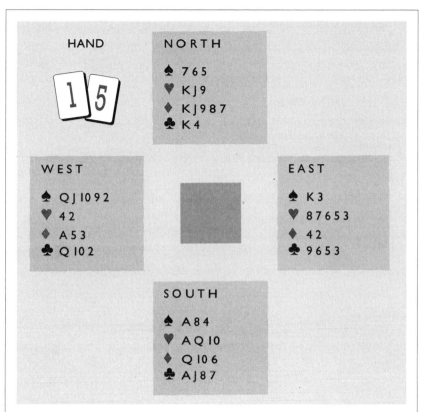

HAND 15

NORTH
♠ 7 6 5
♥ K J 9
♦ K J 9 8 7
♣ K 4

WEST
♠ Q J 10 9 2
♥ 4 2
♦ A 5 3
♣ Q 10 2

EAST
♠ K 3
♥ 8 7 6 5 3
♦ 4 2
♣ 9 6 5 3

SOUTH
♠ A 8 4
♥ A Q 10
♦ Q 10 6
♣ A J 8 7

the ace of diamonds) thus defeating the Three No Trump contract. This hand shows how a Defender with an almost useless hand can have a crucial role in defeating a contract.

THE OPENING LEAD

The opening lead has been the subject of countless books and a great deal of learned discussion over the years. It is impossible always to get right, but it can often be the difference between a contract made or broken, and the Defender making the lead, as Omar Sharif says, has only the development of the auction to provide him with the clues he needs to find the right card. There are, however, certain guidelines which can help immensely. I am not usually one who likes to stick too closely to rules, but unless you know what they are, you do not know how far you can stray from them.

Here they are:

<u>Lead your partner's suit:</u> if your partner has mentioned a suit during the auction, lead it.

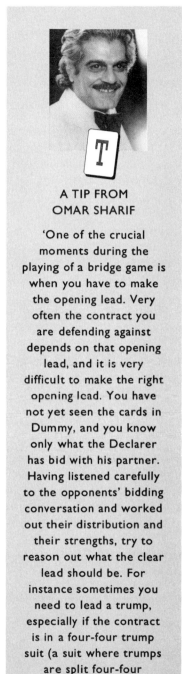

A TIP FROM OMAR SHARIF

'One of the crucial moments during the playing of a bridge game is when you have to make the opening lead. Very often the contract you are defending against depends on that opening lead, and it is very difficult to make the right opening lead. You have not yet seen the cards in Dummy, and you know only what the Declarer has bid with his partner. Having listened carefully to the opponents' bidding conversation and worked out their distribution and their strengths, try to reason out what the clear lead should be. For instance sometimes you need to lead a trump, especially if the contract is in a four-four trump suit (a suit where trumps are split four-four between Declarer and Dummy) and you have strength in the opponents' first suit bid.'

Don't lead a suit bid by your opponents: even if the contract ended up in another suit or in no trumps, steer clear of suits bid by Declarer's side, unless it was a conventional bid, of course, or unless your own hand *tells* you the lead is right.

Lead your longest suit against no trumps, or if two suits are the same length, lead your strongest suit.

Once you have decided on the suit to lead, consider which card to play.

Lead from the top of a sequence: if you hold ♦ K Q J, lead the king. If you hold ♠ J 10 9, lead the jack. That is a safe lead because it is unlikely to lose your partnership a trick, and partner may well recognise it for what it is, and lead back to your sequence when the opportunity arises.

In your suit or your partner's suit, lead the fourth highest in the suit: (♥ Q 9 6 4 2), although if you do not have four cards, lead the top of a doubleton (K 7) or the top of touching high cards (Q J 5), or the lowest of three (J 7 3).

Lead the top of a three card sequence: (K Q J 9 5), the top of an interior sequence: (K 10 9 8 4) or the top of a broken sequence: (J 10 8 5 2). Lead the ace from (A K). Otherwise, lead low – your fourth best card in a suit.

These general guidelines apply when defending against both No Trumps and suit contracts, although when defending against suit contracts, you have other options as well. It may be worth looking at a lead from a short suit, especially from a singleton to increase the chances of a ruff later on. In your own or your partner's suit, lead the ace if you have it, rather than any other card. And if everything else looks dangerous, lead trumps.

Finding the right opening lead every time is, as you can see, something that even a Hercule Poirot or a Sherlock Holmes would find difficult, but there are usually a few clues and rules that can help you. As I have said before, your first choice should be your partner's suit. Do not try to guess or intuit the opening lead. I once used to play with somebody who thought his play was full of imagination and flair. Before leading he gazed at the ceiling for inspiration instead of reviewing the bidding. He helped make more contracts as a Defender than he ever did as Declarer.

SECOND HAND PLAYS LOW

There are several simple tips which can help a Defender in doubt about the best card to play. The first of these is the principle that second hand plays low. If you are the second player to a trick, there is usually no particular need to try to win it for your partnership. It is often better to wait and see what Declarer does, as your partner will play the fourth card and keeping Declarer in suspense until then is often a winning strategy. That means even if you have a card which could win the trick, you should normally play low as second hand unless you have some other sign to guide you. If, for example, playing a high card would defeat the contract, then play it, but consider this simple example:

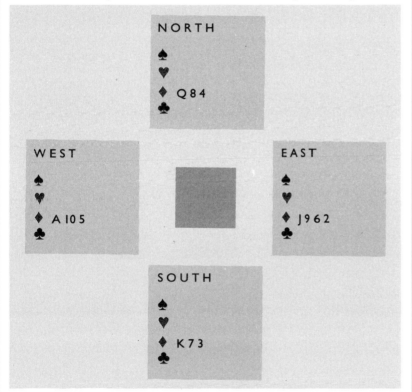

HAND

diamonds only

Note: The cards in Hands 16, 17 and 18 are unevenly distributed between the players because only one suit is shown per hand.

If Declarer (South) leads his three towards Dummy's queen, you may be tempted to play your ace to win the trick. But if you do, Dummy will play a low card, and both his king and queen will be established as winners. If you play low and let him win with the queen, you still have your ace of diamonds but his king is now trapped by it. In defence it is always more satisfying to win a trick which contains at least one of Declarer's potential winners. Using up an ace, which will win anyway, on a trick which only contains a three and a four from Declarer is often a waste of power. They say aces were made to take kings. They may have been right. Having said that, it is obviously dangerous to duck with an ace when Declarer has a singleton. The advantages and disadvantages of second hand plays low need to be weighed up according to the hand.

THIRD HAND PLAYS HIGH

Simple tip number two is an extension of number one. If you are the third hand in the trick, it means two things. Firstly, it means that your partner has led, and secondly it means that you are the last player on your side to play. Both facts are significant in deciding how you should play, and the general rule is, play high.

Let us take this example:

HAND

clubs only

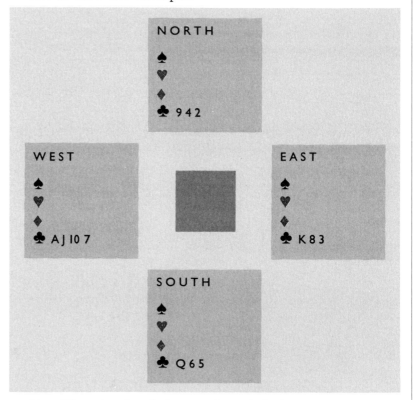

East-West is the defence. West led the seven of clubs on the first trick. Partner's lead will be a potentially good suit for the defence, so when you are the third hand to play, you must assume that partner is expecting you to play your highest card. In this case, Dummy plays the two (second hand low) and East has the choice of the king or the three. Now, although he does not know where the ace is, he still plays the king, either to win the trick or to force South to play the ace to win it. The king actually wins, and by returning a club back to West, the Defenders can take the next two club tricks as well, and a third if Declarer does not ruff. If East had played low on that first club trick, Declarer would have made at least one club trick – one more than he was entitled to.

COVER AN HONOUR WITH AN HONOUR

This is the third simple tip. Like most rules or tips in bridge, it does not apply every time, but covering an honour with an honour is almost always the correct way in which a Defender can promote smaller cards in his or partner's hand.

HAND

18

spades only

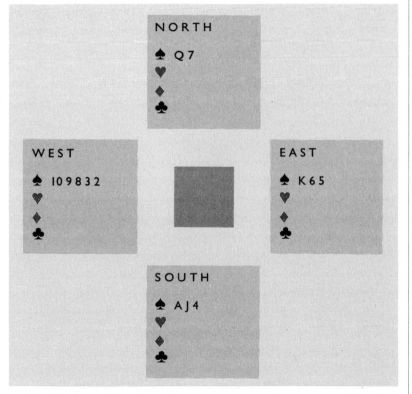

In this hand, if East does not cover the queen of spades led from Dummy with his king, the Declarer will make

three spade tricks, with his queen, jack and ace. If East puts up his king, even though Declarer will win the trick with his ace, East restricts Declarer to two spade tricks, as the ten of spades in his partner's hand is promoted to a winner by the playing of East's king. The point of covering an honour with an honour is therefore to force Declarer to use up two honours to capture one from the defence, and thereby promote winning tricks for your side. If there are no tricks to promote on your side, then it is worth looking again to see whether following the advice of this third tip is entirely correct. Even at a second glance, it usually is. However it should be mentioned that if Dummy has two touching honours it is usually correct to cover the second of them.

SIGNALS

Declarer can see all 26 cards that he can use to make his contract, but each Defender can only see 13 friendly cards: the ones he holds. So each Defender must signal carefully to his partner, so that they can co-operate as a team. By sharing information, they can hope to defeat the contract. If they keep all their secrets to themselves or are unclear in their messages, the Declarer's chances become much stronger. The signals are in the cards played, of course, not in any scratching of noses or pulling of earlobes to convey secret information. Wishy-washy and half-hearted signals are a mistake. You must always signal as clearly as possible to your partner when you want to get a particular message across. As a general rule, a high card played says you like the suit in question, and a low card says you do not like it. Make your signals crystal clear. Don't let your partner misinterpret the cards you are playing. And in this context it is only sensible to play the highest card you can afford (without costing a trick).

Let us take a look at the hand on the opposite page.

The contract is Five Diamonds by South. Nobody else bid. East looks at his hand and realises he has two or three heart winners. West has the ace of trumps, so the best chance for the defence is in the heart suit. West leads the jack of clubs, the top of a sequence in her longest suit. South wins the trick, and plays trumps. He leads the king,

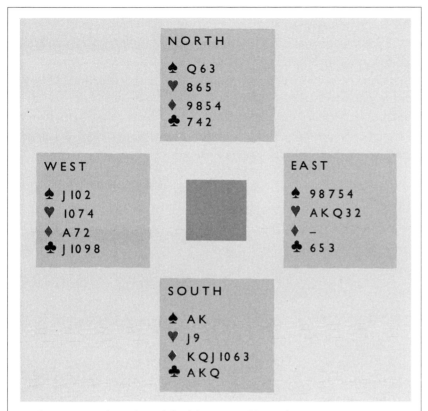

NORTH
♠ Q 63
♥ 865
♦ 9854
♣ 742

WEST
♠ J 10 2
♥ 10 7 4
♦ A 7 2
♣ J 10 9 8

EAST
♠ 98754
♥ AKQ32
♦ –
♣ 653

SOUTH
♠ AK
♥ J 9
♦ KQJ 10 6 3
♣ AKQ

and West takes it with his ace. East has no trumps, so must discard something which will signal to his partner that he wants him to play a heart.

This is the key. If East thinks, 'Apart from my honours, I have only the three and the two, so I will signal with the three to show I want a heart led back.' What is likely to happen? Once West sees East's little three of hearts, she will think, 'Well, that discard was so small, it must mean that partner does not like hearts at all. I'll steer clear of them, and play another club.' The contract would then be made when South has the chance to throw away a heart on the queen of spades and the defence would have failed.

If, on the other hand, East reasons that with one diamond trick already made, they only need two more tricks to defeat the contract, and therefore he has one more heart winner than he needs, he should feel confident about throwing one of his honours on the diamond trick. And to make the point absolutely clear, why not the ace? West could not possibly mistake that signal. Then West would surely lead a heart, East would take two tricks with his king and queen, and the contract would go down.

Bidding is a conversation between two partners, and so is defence. In the first example East wanted to scream to West to lead a heart, but instead he just whispered. The three of hearts was just a tickle to attract attention. In the second example, the ace was a slap which West could not ignore. Always give your partner a slap rather than a tickle, because unlike in life, your partner will appreciate it.

HAND

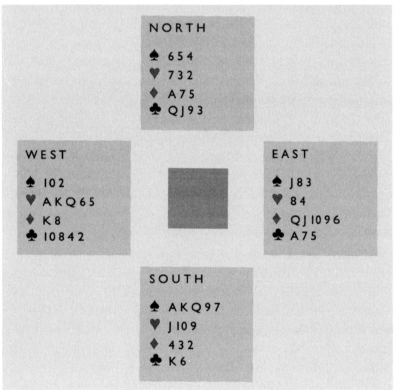

NORTH
♠ 654
♥ 732
♦ A75
♣ QJ93

WEST
♠ 102
♥ AKQ65
♦ K8
♣ 10842

EAST
♠ J83
♥ 84
♦ QJ1096
♣ A75

SOUTH
♠ AKQ97
♥ J109
♦ 432
♣ K6

This hand illustrates a similar case: the contract was Two Spades. The opening lead by West was the obviously correct ace of hearts, and he followed it up with the king and queen. On the third round, East needed to discard, and wanted to make her diamond holding clear to her partner. But which card to play? With four sequential diamonds, the correct answer was to play the highest, the queen, which proved an excellent choice, because it told her partner, 'I have the queen, the jack and the 10.' It turned out that West had the king of diamonds and now led it. The king was taken by North's ace, but it set up East's jack and 10 as winners. The defence could later win their ace of clubs, thus defeating the Two Spade contract by one trick (three heart tricks, two diamond tricks and one club trick). This was excellent defence. If East had discarded the nine of diamonds it might not have been enough to get the exact message across, and discarding a low club to say she did not like clubs would also have been less informative. <u>Always signal clearly what you like before letting partner know what you do not like.</u>

UNDERSTAND DECLARER'S POSITION

Another very important strategy for a Defender is to try to look at a problem from the Declarer's point of view, to try to enter the Declarer's mind and to try to understand what his feelings and problems are in making a contract. The trained saboteur often crosses enemy lines to try to discover its weak points. He wants to know exactly where to place his bomb. There is no point in using your most powerful card where it is not needed, or in throwing a hand grenade where only a truckload of dynamite will do the trick. By trying to put yourself into the mind of Declarer, you can time your card play to afford him the maximum difficulty, and never let him off the hook.

Here is an example of such a strategy. It is extreme, but clear and, I believe, very useful. Imagine you pick up the following not unattractive hand and are just thinking about which suit to bid:

♠ 3   ♥ A 10 7 4   ♦ A 9 8 7   ♣ A 8 3 2

Before you have a chance to bid, the man on your right bids, firmly and most surprisingly, Seven Spades. The auction is over before it began. You wonder what sort of madness must have possessed him because with your three aces and one spade (which means he cannot have 13 spades) you know he could not make Seven Spades. So you Double (you would, wouldn't you?). You lead the ace of hearts. Dummy is:

♠ –   ♥ K Q 9 6 5   ♦ K Q 6 5   ♣ K Q 7 6

At this point, fate takes a hand. The coffee you had previously ordered finally arrives and the clumsy waiter spills the coffee all over both Dummy and your partner's hand. Dummy's cards are completely soaked and illegible and your partner's cards as he plays them are equally unclear. But this doesn't bother you too much, after all you are defending against a doubled grand slam, with two aces still in your hand. You continue regardless. Declarer trumps the ace of hearts, and leads the ace of spades. You follow with your three and cards are thrown from Dummy and partner (you can't tell which). However you ask your partner, 'Spades?' To which he replies, 'No Spades.'

So now we know that Declarer has twelve spades, and just one other card. You have two more aces, one of which will definitely be a winner *if*, and only *if*, you can keep the right ace for the final trick when Declarer will play his one mystery card. The moment of truth finally arrives and Declarer, finally exhausted of his spades, plays his last one, the two, on the table. You have in your hand the ace of diamonds and the ace of clubs. Which one do you play and which one do you keep?

A clue: the way to solve this problem is to put yourself into the Declarer's mind. If you do not do this, you have no more than one chance in two of getting it right. But if you review the information you have, (the Seven Spade bid), you might be able to work it out. Remember, he bid Seven Spades and with what seemed to be a great deal of confidence on the very first round of bidding. Yet you know he did not have all 13 spades. You also know that his final card is not an ace — you held the other three — yet still he bid Seven Spades. Why was that?

Try and work it out before you look at the answer.

The way to work out this problem, and many similar ones that will occur in your bridge life, is to think, 'Why did he open Seven Spades and not Six Spades? When would I open Seven Spades?'

The answer surely would be if you saw 13 tricks in your hand, either 13 spades or 11 spades and two aces for example. With 12 spades and no ace, he would normally bid his sure small slam: Six Spades. *Unless* he *thought* he had 13 spades. So you throw away the ace of diamonds and keep the ace of clubs. As long as Declarer was not colour blind, you will have defeated the contract.

DISCARDS AND FALSE CARDS

There is one final vital aspect of defence which we need to discuss, and that is the art of discarding and false cards. Many players have great difficulty, especially when they are starting out, with the way to make their discards helpful and useful. The purpose of every discard should be to clarify your holdings, your likes and your dislikes, to your partner. For example, when you do not like a suit, you should discard as many of that suit as possible so that your partner understands your feelings clearly. It is often correct to finish discarding from one suit before you go on to the next, rather than muddling matters by discarding a few cards from one suit and a few from another.

Use your imagination. Sometimes you may be defending what appears to be a hopeless cause. With no chance to beat Declarer that you can see, you feel like giving up. Don't. Now is the time to have some fun. You have nothing to lose. Throw away an ace, a king or lead a strange card! Try something really unusual. It certainly cannot do any harm, and, who knows, there may be times when you strike gold, even if only by luck!

Let me show you what I think is the finest example of an imaginative defensive play that I have ever come across. It was played by the great Swiss international player Jean Besse, and although it may be hard to understand and even more difficult to repeat in your own play, it is worth studying as the supreme example of what brilliant and innovative discarding can do to what appears to be an invincible contract. Look at the hand on page 74.

The contract is Six Spades, a contract reached after South had bid hearts along the way. West led his singleton heart. South played the ace from Dummy, feeling correctly that West's lead in his bid suit was probably a singleton, thus giving up on the heart finesse and relying instead on the position of the king of spades. Bad luck on West, but a good lead that did not quite work. At this point it was Jean's turn to play, sitting in East's chair. For a moment let us try to imagine how his mind must have been working at this stage.

Besse saw immediately that if he played a low heart, the

```
              ♠ Q J 4
   HAND       ♥ A Q J 7
    21        ♦ K Q 5
              ♣ K 9 8

♠ 8 5 3         N          ♠ K 6
♥ 2                        ♥ K 8 4
♦ 10 8 4 3   W     E       ♦ J 7 6 2
♣ 10 7 6 4 2    S          ♣ Q J 5 3

              ♠ A 10 9 7 2
              ♥ 10 9 6 5 3
              ♦ A 9
              ♣ A
```

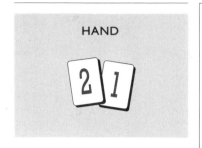

HAND

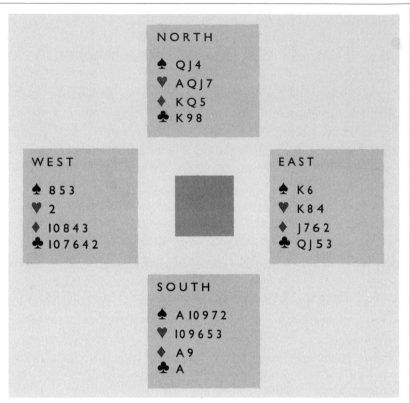

NORTH
- ♠ Q J 4
- ♥ A Q J 7
- ♦ K Q 5
- ♣ K 9 8

WEST
- ♠ 8 5 3
- ♥ 2
- ♦ 1 0 8 4 3
- ♣ 1 0 7 6 4 2

EAST
- ♠ K 6
- ♥ K 8 4
- ♦ J 7 6 2
- ♣ Q J 5 3

SOUTH
- ♠ A 1 0 9 7 2
- ♥ 1 0 9 6 5 3
- ♦ A 9
- ♣ A

Declarer's next move would be to play the queen of spades from Dummy and take the spade finesse. He knew that the finesse would work because he was looking at the king in his own hand. He also knew that Declarer was about to make his slam. He recognised from the opening lead that his partner had a singleton heart, but wanted to make the position more confusing, wanted to blur the message, to Declarer's eyes at least. He knew that if he played low Declarer would surely make his contract. So it was time for him to do something imaginative, something spectacular, something that might perhaps deter Declarer from the winning line. What did he do? He threw his king of hearts away under Dummy's ace! Look what effect this had.

When Declarer saw the king of hearts played, he was astonished. He had assumed from the lead that it was West who had the singleton heart, but who would throw a king under an ace unless he had no choice? And if the singleton heart was in East's hand, he could no longer afford the spade finesse, because if West had the king of spades and three hearts, when the spade finesse was taken West would win with the king and lead a heart for East to ruff and so defeat the contract. If East had the trump king he might win an undeserved trick with it but could do no further damage. It was therefore surely right to give up the trump finesse and play the ace of spades and another, before a heart was ruffed.

So as a result of Jean Besse's brilliant false card, Declarer gave up the idea of the finesse and in starting to draw trumps, played a low spade from Dummy towards his ace, and then another round of spades. Much to his astonishment, it was East who not only took this trick with the king, but then led a heart for his partner to ruff and defeat the contract. Declarer was fooled, but who would not have been? The whole manoeuvre was brilliant. Besse did it because he could not see any other way to defeat the contract except by doing something drastic which would make Declarer go astray. The speed with which he analysed the options and made that particular play amazes me, because he could not sit there, and ponder. A play like that has to be made at an even tempo in order to be successful in its deception.

Naturally I do not expect you to reach the level of Jean Besse. I am sure that I could never have come up with such a master stroke so quickly, but just to appreciate the beauty of the play is enough. Every card tells a story, they say, but some stories are better than others.

In conclusion I would just like to give you an instance of a humorous defensive play called *The Grosvenor Gambit*, named after a Mr Grosvenor who may have been the figment of someone's imagination, or he may not. Grosvenor's speciality was to make defensive plays that for no good reason gave the Declarer an opportunity to make a free trick, one he was not entitled to. The only problem for the Declarer was that he would be so suspicious and so sure that the Defender was not really being so charitable, that he would not take advantage of the play, only to find, at the end of the hand, that the Defender had presented him with just such an opportunity. Grosvenor did this, they say, to annoy the Declarer so much that he remained furious for the remaining hands and made subsequent errors.

Let me show you what I mean.

HAND

spades only

Spades are trumps and are divided:

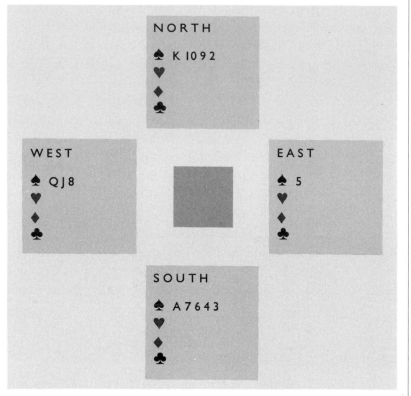

If played normally, after the ace and king are played, West will make a trick with his queen of spades. But Grosvenor on the play of the ace of spades from South would play the queen! This allows Declarer a chance to finesse the jack and lose no tricks! When he followed low on the second round, Declarer would be sure that East started with a jack doubleton, otherwise why would West give up a sure trick; Declarer would play the king and would be furious when he discovered the actual layout. There are many opportunities for this light-hearted play, but BE CAREFUL: you must thoroughly understand the basic rules before you attempt the more bizarre ones.

Defence is the greatest test of a partnership. In the auction you have a chance to talk directly to each other, and to tell each other something about your hand. In Declarer play, one member of the partnership can take a rest while the other half gets on with it. In defence, you have to work with your partner on a strategy that you can only fully develop together as the play evolves. You are playing on your opponent's terms and the odds are likely to be stacked heavily against you in any well-bid contract. A successful defence, using the combined skills and strengths of both Defenders, is one of the most satisfying achievements in an evening of bridge, and it can bring out some of the most exciting and invigorating play of all.

5

HOW TO
BE A WINNER

There is a story of three well known bridge professionals who were playing rubber bridge one evening at a club in London. The fourth player in their party was a wealthy but unskilled lover of the game, who used his money to earn himself the privilege of playing with the world's best. Although the four were not playing for particularly large stakes, by the end of a long evening the three internationals had each made a tidy sum of money, while their wealthy patron had lost a bundle. After the winnings had been sorted out, the three internationals put on their coats and headed out into the cold London rain to try to hail a cab. They stood on the pavement outside, getting wetter and wetter as they waited for a taxi. Finally they decided to start walking and it was at this point that the wealthy loser drove past in his Rolls Royce. 'Look, there goes the pigeon', said one of the shivering professionals to his cold, wet companions. (A pigeon is a player who is seen by the others at the table, especially when playing for money, as the likely loser).

The moral of this story is simple. If you cannot recognise who is the winner and who is the loser, how can you be a winner? There is a saying in rubber bridge that every time you sit down at the table you should ask yourself the question, 'Who is the pigeon here?' If you cannot answer, take care, because the pigeon might be you.

But it is worse to be a palooka. A palooka is somebody who is quite useless at bridge. I hope by now you have graduated beyond the stage of the palooka, but there are some people who persist in being palookas year in year out, not because they are technically incapable of playing cards, but because they do not take the right attitude towards their bridge. The right attitude is not a matter of taking the game incredibly seriously or spending hundreds of pounds on bridge books, videos, computer games and lessons. It is just a matter of making the most of your time at the bridge table, of playing positively and for the fun of the game.

But as in every sport or pastime, winning at bridge is more fun than losing. If you like bridge, and you play regularly, you may not have any ambition to be the world's best, but you still want to be a winner. Being a winner is not necessarily the same as being technically the best player. Winning is a state of mind. I can't bear losing. In rubber bridge the only thing you can lose is money, which is bad enough, but in duplicate bridge, you risk an even worse fate known as the shriek.

Let me explain what the shriek is and how it works. In duplicate bridge, (tournament bridge) each partnership plays the same hands at different tables, and the score is calculated by the relative success of each partnership in playing each hand. By the end of a tournament it may take a little time to work out which partnership emerges as the overall winner, especially if no one partnership has clearly outplayed the rest. So all the partnerships tend to compare scores after the final boards have been played, and score up. While the process of scoring up is going on, you can be sure that sooner or later one team will let out an ear-piercing shriek of victory. The shriek, usually at a decibel level that would shatter a double-glazed window, tells the other partnerships they don't need to bother carrying on calculating their scores, because somebody else, the shriekers' partnership to be precise, has won. This is a most depressing moment for all of those who are not shrieking, and one to be avoided if possible.

There are, however, three known ways of avoiding the awful fate of the shriekee. The first way is to win the tournament, which is of course the most satisfactory solution, but even the best players cannot always guarantee success. The second way, requiring a mental agility which is not always there at the end of a long bridge tournament, is to add up your score faster than anybody else, so that you can make your getaway before the shriek occurs. The third way is to shriek yourself, even if you have not won. This psychic shriek may not be playing strictly fair, but it certainly unnerves your opponents, and for a couple of minutes you are in heaven and they are in hell. Of course, the winners' heaven is even more heavenly when they discover that your shriek was a pre-emptive bid, and that a tournament they thought was lost has actually been won. Enough of losing. Here are some ways to help you win.

WINNING IN THE NO TRUMP WORLD

The quickest route to making a game, as we have already seen, is by making a contract in Three No Trumps. You only need to win nine tricks, and 100 points below the line are yours. That is why the contract is so often attempted, and why no trumps are attractive even for players whose cards seem unsuitable for such a contract. In the UK a weak no trump is often played (12 to 14 points for an opening bid of One No Trump). In the US they tend to play the strong no trump system (15 to 17 points). In Pakistan we sometimes play the mini no trump, which is even weaker than a weak no trump! It does not matter which you play as long as you and your partner are happy. But what hands belong in no trumps? No trump hands are normally part of a family, the family of balanced hands which we have already met. If you have a balanced hand it is usually right to play in no trumps. If both you and your partner have balanced hands, without an eight card major suit fit, then you have the ingredients of a good no trump contract.

WINNING WITH BAD HANDS

We have already seen that if you have 12 to 14 high card points and a balanced hand, then an opening bid of One No Trump is called for. We also know that as Responder to this One No Trump opening with, say 6-11 high card points, we will be in the partscore zone. As Responder with 12 or more points, we are in the game or slam zone. But how do you respond to that opening bid if you have no points at all? How can you turn a hand like that into a winner? Or at least save it from being a big loser?

This hand illustrates the problem, and suggests one of my own answers to what seems to be a frequent dilemma.

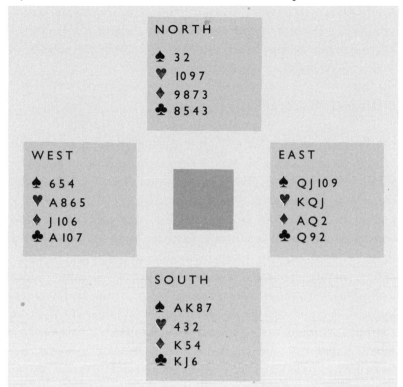

NORTH
♠ 3 2
♥ 10 9 7
♦ 9 8 7 3
♣ 8 5 4 3

WEST
♠ 6 5 4
♥ A 8 6 5
♦ J 10 6
♣ A 10 7

EAST
♠ Q J 10 9
♥ K Q J
♦ A Q 2
♣ Q 9 2

SOUTH
♠ A K 8 7
♥ 4 3 2
♦ K 5 4
♣ K J 6

South opened the bidding One No Trump, indicating his 14 high card points and a balanced hand. West, with only 9 points, passed. North had a problem. North's reasoning probably went something like this: 'My partner has 12 to 14 points, and I have none. That means our opponents have 26 to 28 between them, and as West did not bid, we must assume that most of the points are held by East. I have no points, so I shall say No Bid.' This simple logic is theoretically correct. But unfortunately, theory is not always practicable. After North passed, East inevitably doubled, and North-South failed to make One No Trump doubled, conceding a large penalty point.

North did well up to a point, but could, perhaps, have done better. With barely one third of the total points held by his partnership and the balance of power against him, the best he could do was to look for ways to ward off disaster rather than bury his head in the sand and hope things would have changed when he came up for air. East was bound to double One No Trump if North passed, so what could North do? He might have bid Two Diamonds. Why? Because although East can double One No Trump for penalties, if he doubled Two Diamonds it would usually be taken as a takeout double – asking West to bid his best suit – thus if North had bid Two Diamonds he might have avoided the disaster.

BIDDING MESSAGES

All bids should ideally tell your partner whether you want him to keep bidding or not. Like traffic lights, bids should signal red, amber or green, so that you know when to stop and when to go on.

The red light bids are called sign-off bids. You do not want your partner to bid any further. If he shoots the red light, he will end up in trouble. The amber light bids are called invitational bids. These are bids when you are not quite sure about the correct level to play in, and you will leave it to your partner to decide. The green light bids are called forcing bids. Your partner must reply. If your partner does not respond to a forcing by saying something, anything, you can, for once, break the rule about partnership harmony. Give him or her hell in the nicest possible way!

SIGN-OFF BIDS

North's recommended Two Diamond response described in the last hand (to South's One No Trump) is a sign-off bid. It tells partner that he should not bid any higher, It is a bid which solves the problem that my dry-cleaning lady was experiencing in Chapter Two about knowing when to stop (see page 28). Equally any Pass is a sign-off bid. Other sign-off responses to a One No Trump bid include any bid which leaves the partnership in game, that is Three No Trumps, Four Spades, Four Hearts, Five Diamonds or Five Clubs. The Responder (North in the last hand) knows so much about Opener's hand from a One No Trump bid that he can often decide by simple arithmetic that the partnership has enough points for game and go straight there. No further discussion is required.

Any two level bid, except the Stayman Two Clubs, after

a One No Trump bid, is also a sign-off bid. It tells the Opener that the partnership cannot get to game, and that Responder would prefer to play in a suit contract rather than in a no trump contract, usually because of the distribution of his hand, but sometimes because of extreme weakness, as in the last hand.

INVITATIONAL BIDS

Obviously any opening bid short of a grand slam is invitational at least in part. Response bids are more subtle in their meaning, although the zones in which the bids fall usually make the bidder's intention clear.

All opening suit bids at the one level are invitational; similarly as we have seen, an opening bid of One No Trump is invitational.

Invitational bids say to your partner, 'Look, I'm not quite sure about the level we ought to be at, although I am fairly confident about the suit. Why don't you decide?' In response to One No Trump, the most obvious invitational bid is Two No Trumps. That says, 'Yes I like what I am hearing, but my hand is a borderline one. If you have 14 points, we can get to game, but if you only have 12, you should pass.' And that leaves the decision up to the Opener. If you look back to hand number three in Chapter Two there was an invitational sequence following South's One No Trump bid.

FORCING BIDS

Forcing bids are invitational in that they do not conclude the auction, but they are forcing because they insist that partner bids again. A Pass will not be good enough. In answer to an opening bid of One No Trump, there are various forcing bids, Two Clubs, Three Clubs, Three Diamonds, Three Hearts and Three Spades. Two Clubs is Stayman, asking whether there is a four-four fit in a major suit. You cannot put an end to a conventional bid until the information asked for has been given. Three Clubs, Three Diamonds, Three Hearts and Three Spades are recognisable as forcing bids because they take the bidding up by two levels without going all the way to game. What the

A TIP FROM OMAR SHARIF

'Be very careful with doubles, especially with partscores. In low level partscores make sure you have good trump tricks on your side. Don't forget that if you have lots of points in your hand and opponents are bidding, they are bidding on distribution. Distribution is a very dangerous thing and can be more important actually than points. Sometimes you have a lot of points but they have the distribution and the contract does not come down in spite of all the aces and kings that you have. So make sure first of all that you have trump tricks before doubling an opponent in a partscore, not just high cards. Otherwise you risk the fate of conceding a contract doubled and made, which is very unpleasant.'

Responder is saying is, 'We have at least game points. Do you want to play the contract in a suit or in No Trumps?' He does not want the Opener to stop short of game, so the bid is forcing the Opener to choose between the suit and No Trumps. And if we go back to the very first sequence we looked at in Chapter One on page 13, Responder's bid in a new suit in response to an opening bid is forcing. By contrast however, almost all simple raises of partner's suit, or no trump bids, either by Opener or Responder, are non-forcing. So again, looking at that very first hand, Opener's simple raise of his partner's suit to Two Hearts was not forcing.

The most common invitational sequences come from raising partner's suit, or bidding no trumps. Unless a forcing sequence has already been established, these bids are generally invitational.

Look at this hand:

♠ A K J 8   ♥ 9 7 3   ♦ A Q 4   ♣ 9 5 4

With 14 points and a balanced hand the natural opening bid is One No Trump. Partner responded with Two Spades. Now, you know that this is a sign-off bid, saying that partner wants to play at the two level, but at the same time it is tempting to raise the bid to Three Spades. Resist the temptation, because partner is likely to have a hand like this:

♠ Q 10 9 7 5 2   ♥ 8 6 5   ♦ K J   ♣ J 10

Two Spades is possible, Three Spades is not, because you have five losers, in Three Hearts and Two Clubs.

When you have a relatively weak hand as a Responder, as opposed to no points as illustrated earlier you can still turn this to your advantage if you know the techniques of being a winner. The hand opposite does not look particularly exciting at first glance; but even an average hand like this can become a potent weapon.

Imagine you are in North's position. Your partner, South, has dealt and opened the bidding with One No Trump. A balanced hand with 12-14 points is an obvious One No Trump bid. West doubles. This is a typical

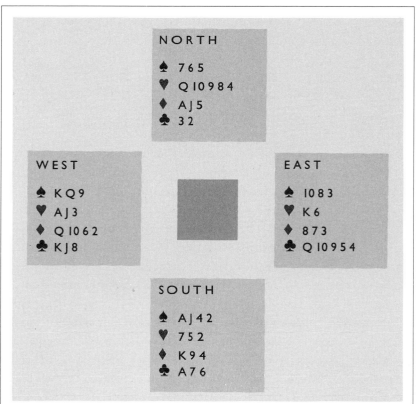

NORTH
- ♠ 765
- ♥ Q 10 9 8 4
- ♦ A J 5
- ♣ 3 2

WEST
- ♠ K Q 9
- ♥ A J 3
- ♦ Q 10 6 2
- ♣ K J 8

EAST
- ♠ 10 8 3
- ♥ K 6
- ♦ 8 7 3
- ♣ Q 10 9 5 4

SOUTH
- ♠ A J 4 2
- ♥ 7 5 2
- ♦ K 9 4
- ♣ A 7 6

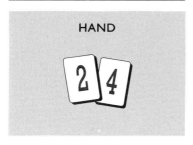

penalty double, where West has not the distribution to bid Two in any suit, but has more than enough points to have opened the bidding if South had not already done so. A takeout double, by contrast, says to your partner, 'Bid your best suit. I may not have enough points to get game but I've got all the other suits covered.' It is important not to confuse a takeout double with a penalty double, especially as both are bid with the same word. However, the differences are clear enough. A takeout double happens when your opponents are bidding suits and are still in the partscore zone and when you have not previously bid. A double is a penalty double when your opponents are already in the game zone, or when your side has already bid, or when, as here, they are in No Trumps. A takeout double is virtually a forcing bid. Your partner really ought not to pass unless there is further action from your opponents first. At any rate in this case, all West is doing is showing he has a pretty good hand. (See glossary for further definitions of takeout and penalty doubles).

With seven high card points and another point for

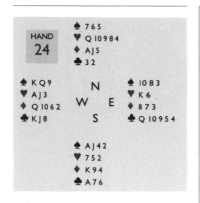

HAND 24

♠ 765
♥ Q 10 9 8 4
♦ A J 5
♣ 3 2

♠ K Q 9
♥ A J 3
♦ Q 10 6 2
♣ K J 8

N
W E
S

♠ 10 8 3
♥ K 6
♦ 8 7 3
♣ Q 10 9 5 4

♠ A J 4 2
♥ 7 5 2
♦ K 9 4
♣ A 7 6

length in hearts, North has several options. The text books would suggest Two Hearts, and that is certainly reasonable. It looks likely that you can make Two Hearts, although there is really no chance of making game either in hearts or no trumps. So most people would bid Two Hearts, and make it. Sixty solid points below the line. But for those who like a little adventure, there are other ways to play this hand and perhaps, make a much larger profit.

When I say, 'almost everybody would bid Two Hearts', I mean that although it is normal, I wouldn't. In fact, when I actually came across this hand and was playing North, I did not bid Two Hearts. I knew my partner well enough to trust him to leave the mad end of the bidding spectrum to me, so I bid Two Clubs. This spread, as I intended, a certain amount of confusion among my opponents. Was I using Stayman and looking for a four-four major suit fit? Did I really mean clubs when East, as it turned out, had five of them? It was in fact a simple psychic bid, meant to cause a little disruption to the thought processes of the opposition. Because of the bidding and because clubs was my shortest suit, I knew clubs were likely to be East's longest suit, and if he doubled I could bid my heart suit later. Perhaps East-West would misread the situation and double my hearts as well. And what did I have to lose? The worst that could happen was that I would play the hand in Two Clubs and go a few down non-vulnerable. East, looking at his clubs, did double. South passed and so did West. At this point I bid Two Hearts, which was where I had always wanted to be. East passed, but West, scenting blood, reasoned that if East could double me in Two Clubs, he could double me in Two Hearts, thinking my bid was an attempt to escape. So the contract ended up as Two Hearts Doubled, which we made, and Two Hearts Doubled is game, $(30+30=60\times2=120 + 50=170)$. Sometimes average hands are not so average after all.

I do not recommend the principle of psychic bidding to everybody, but at times like this it can turn a humdrum hand into something quite exciting. That's the fun of the game, and it can be profitable too.

THREE CLOSELY GUARDED SECRETS FROM THE EXPERTS

How does the mind of a bridge expert work? What is the difference between a solid, competent and reasonably successful bridge player and a winning player? I will let you into some of the most closely guarded secrets of the top international players. I will not give away all of them, or one day you may meet me at the bridge table and beat me, but there are three that I can pass on, which will make your play more consistently effective, and may on occasions make you join the ranks of the brilliant.

The first secret: your psychology. Bridge is not a game for automatons. Although there is a great deal of logical thought in the bidding and the play at bridge, a computer will never be a match for a top bridge player, because there is more to bridge than logic. I have not yet seen a computer that reaches a particularly high skill level, and I do not believe that the logical thought processes of a computer are enough to compete with the human and sometimes illogical skills of the top bridge players. Your opponents are human beings, the game was invented by human beings and the way to win is to play like a human being, sometimes making what appear to be deliberate errors, and sometimes playing in a way that a computer would not accept as logical, and therefore possible. A good bridge player plays through feelings as much as knowledge. Don't subjugate those feelings in an effort to play like a computer. Use tactics that are not obviously logical, but that can be deadly.

A winning player must have what we call table presence. This is not only the ability to sense the opponents' problems, strengths and weaknesses, a knack which takes practice, but the ability to create an aura of confidence and strength so that your opponents respect you. When I started playing bridge I found it helped to make people think that I was a very lucky player. Luck is where you make it, and a top bridge player is no luckier than a beginner. But opponents are more ready to lose to someone who is lucky and skilful. I do not believe in luck in the long run, but a good player can make his luck look like skilful play. He can also sometimes make skilful play look like luck, so that his opponents believe they are up

against not only a good player, but one for whom the cards fall consistently well. People who think their opponents are lucky must imagine that they themselves are unlucky. Unlucky players become losers. But bear in mind what Gary Player said when he was accused of being a lucky golfer. He said, 'Yes, and the more I practise, the luckier I get.' As in all games, you go through periods when you feel in top form, where everything seems to go right, and at other times it seems the gods are conspiring against you.

My second secret: the way we treat our partners. We all know that the etiquette of bridge demands that at the table all players remain calm and controlled in their bidding and play, but we all also know of examples of players who forget this simple courtesy. All too often more experienced players lose their patience with less expert partners, which is not only discouraging for the beginners but also does nothing whatsoever to help the better players improve their game. We all appreciate encouragement from our partners: it makes us feel we can become winners. Furthermore, my experience in teaching bridge has made me realise how much I learn about my own game by teaching others. If we treat our partners, at whatever level of skill and performance they may be, with positive encouragement rather than bullying them into our way of thinking, we will become better players, *and* we will achieve better results.

I cannot overemphasise the importance of treating your partner well.

My third secret: make use of the hesitations of your opponents. It is absolutely wrong to use your partner's hesitations or uneven tempo in any way that could possibly be thought to influence your play, but there is nothing wrong in taking advantage of your opponents' uncertainties although naturally you do so at your own risk. For example, why is your opponent taking a long time to lead against your no trump contract? Is it because he has no easy lead, no five card suit to lead, for example? It quite likely is that he has a balanced hand, perhaps with honours in each suit, and he is finding it hard to choose the right card or suit to lead. The hesitation has told us a little more about one of the opposing hands, information we can use as play develops.

What if the bidding starts on your right with One No

Trump? You are holding a bad hand, so you pass. On your left, your opponent raises to Two No Trumps, an invitational bid suggesting game might be possible. Back to your right hand opponent, and he pauses to think about the matter for a long while. Finally he says Three No Trumps, bidding game. Now why did he take so long to bid? It will nearly always be because he does not have a maximum One No Trump – he probably had 12 or 13 points only, and if his partner was not strong enough to take the bidding straight into the game zone, then he is in a doubtful contract which is going to be very closely fought. Now you should concentrate very hard on the play, because it is going to be a photo-finish. Maybe you should double. Use your opponents' hesitation to the full, but remember, they will be making use of your hesitations as well. He who hesitates is lost.

Here is a hand which combines psychology and table presence, the traits of a winner:

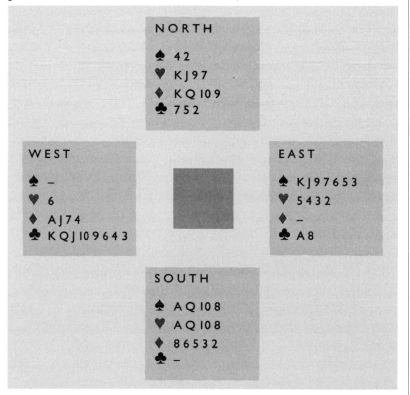

HAND

Although North holds a balanced hand, it only has nine points and all the other players have a void. The bidding started with the dealer, East. Let's listen in on the players'

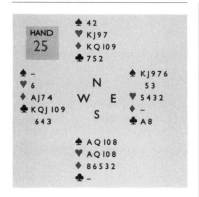

thoughts as they compete in the auction.

East: I have a long spade suit, but only eight high card points. Even if I add three more points for the length of my spades, that is not enough for a standard opening bid. However, I do want to tell my partner about my spades, and I also want to restrict my opponents' room for manoeuvre in the auction. This is ideal for a pre-emptive bid, (a bid made at a higher level than the points alone allow). Three Spades.

South: I have 12 high card points, including the ace and queen in East's pre-emptive suit, spades. But I do not have enough strength to get into the bidding at Four Hearts which is what I'd have to do, nor do I have the right distribution to try a takeout double. But the auction is not over yet, and although I will have to pass this time, I may have a chance to act later. Pass.

West: East's pre-emptive bid seems to have served its purpose of disrupting the bidding, but it may have disrupted our side as well! I'm not sure who can make what, but who knows, I might make Five Clubs, but go down in Three Spades. What the hell, Five Clubs.

North: This auction is over my head. Pass.

East: I did not expect my pre-emptive bid to bring that reaction from partner. Five Clubs is a strange bid. She obviously does not like spades at all, and by jumping a level in a new suit, she is telling me that her clubs are very good. I have a very good hand in support of clubs and if partner can make five, I can contribute. Perhaps our partnership can even make a slam. But as I do not know, I had better not take the risk. Five Clubs gives us game anyway. Pass. (These thoughts have taken a noticeably long time).

South: Pass.

The contract was therefore Five Clubs. Now the problem for North is what card to lead to begin the defence of the contract. Let us listen to him again.

North: What on earth am I going to lead? My partner didn't bid so there are no clues there. I could lead a heart and hope that partner has the ace, or I could make the standard lead of a high diamond, the top of the sequence, which is probably the safest. Spades are obviously dangerous, because Dummy has lots of them and Declarer may be void, and clubs are trumps. (The rules for leading are explained on page 63).

So North led the king of diamonds, which Declarer won with the ace, and East-West made the contract when West remembered to trump two diamonds in Dummy, rather than to draw trumps. However there was one lead which would have defeated the contract and the clue to making it was there, if North had turned his attention to the length of time that East had spent in making up her mind about her final bid, a pass. He should have thought along these lines:

North: What on earth am I going to lead? Let's think about how the bidding went. Why did East pause for so long before passing? It couldn't have been to go back to spades, that was obviously no go. The only reason could have been because she thought that Six Clubs was a possibility. Now I've got nine high card points, and even if South has none, East-West cannot have more than 31 between them, which would not normally put them in the slam zone. I know from the pre-empt that East has got a lot of spades, and from West's response that she has very few spades, otherwise West would have bid Four Spades. I also know that West has a lot of clubs. So what else would help them reach a small slam in clubs? Obviously, East has a singleton or a void somewhere, and is counting on ruffing from the beginning to make the contract. So that tells me what to lead: a club to prevent at least one of Dummy's ruffs. Who knows, it may bring down the contract. I hope my partner forgives me if I am dreaming.

With these thoughts North would lead the two of clubs and take one of Dummy's two trumps out of play. The contract would be defeated and North would have used the hesitation of his opponent to his advantage. Some people might have thought the trump lead lucky, but you can see that it was the result of careful thought. There is always an element of good fortune in a game, but winners make the most of it, and often create their own luck.

WHAT MAKES A WINNING PLAYER?

People often suggest to me that to be a good bridge player, to be a winner, you need intuition. They have even said that one reason why bridge is so popular with women is because it is an intuitive game. I do not agree. Bridge is a game of logic and clarity coupled with intuition. As we have seen, there are times when you can sum up the evidence of the bidding and the play to work out where a particular card is sitting waiting to fall, and others where your intuition helps you to the winning play, like a lead based on an opponents' hesitation when bidding. You need both logic and intuition. When you watch a great golfer going for an intuitive shot which you might think impossible, it is highly likely that he has practised it hundreds of times and knows that it is possible. The same thing applies in bridge. Bid according to the rules and conventions. Lead according to what you have worked out about the hands held. Play the way you have learnt from practising. And then use your intuition. The combination makes the game fascinating.

One thing I have noticed which is common to all the top bridge players is that they often have a highly orderly and logical mind. It is interesting also to note that they tend to have a good vocabulary (even though the bidding language only has a handful of words), and are excellent at spelling. Generally, the top bridge players are intelligent (although not always), but it is not necessarily the sort of intelligence which stores up thousands of facts for later use. It is the sort of intelligence which enables them to perceive a problem clearly, and work out the solution. Ask a bridge player for directions to a destination, and you will get a clear and easy to follow answer. There is no intuition in this. It is a matter of understanding the situation, working out what is needed and passing on the required information as concisely and simply as possible. It is a matter of communication. And communication is one of the fundamentals of bridge, and something that winners at the game are good at.

Conventions, as we have seen, are part of that communication process, even though they can be misunderstood. There are a few conventions, reputedly real but more likely imagined, which are worth mentioning mainly for their comic value. For example, there is Liar's Blackwood. One team I played in used to be renowned as a team of overbidders. Whether they followed my lead or I grew to be like my team-mates, I am not sure, but certainly

I have always had a tendency to climb up the bidding ladder at a faster rate than most. So if we had already overbid, and partner used Blackwood to find out about our aces, there were members of the team who would hide one of their aces. The bidding would go something like this: East: One Spade, West: Three Spades. East: Four No Trumps (checking for aces), West: Five Diamonds (one ace). East: Five Hearts (this is your last chance to confess if you were hiding an ace. Well?), West: Six Spades (Okay, I admit two aces, and I hope you make it). This convention should be reserved for serious overbidders, because otherwise it can ruin partnership trust.

Similarly, there is Irish Stayman. Here, Responder bids Two Clubs without either major suit. His purpose is not to find a fit but to satisfy his curiosity as to whether one of the partnership holds a major suit..

Or the Polish Western Cue Bid. The normal Western Cue Bid is an overcall of three of your right hand opponent's suit. It annouces a good hand with a solid suit and asks partner to bid Three No Trumps if he has a stop in Opener's suit. (A stop is a card which will prevent your opponents reeling out their winners in that suit). This bid also implies a long running suit of your own. You are therefore hoping to play in Three No Trumps.

The Polish Western Cue Bid of three of your right hand opponent's suit announces a stop in the suit, but asks partner if he by any chance has a solid suit somewhere!

In the end, the only way to be a winner is to play. I play whenever I can. I play partly to get better and partly because I love it. Whenever you think you have mastered the game, it strikes back and reminds you that you don't know so much after all. But there will be many occasions when you are the person who lets out the shriek of victory, especially if you believe you can.

THE MYSTERY OF BRIDGE

ORIGINS, DEVELOPMENT AND SOME CHAMPIONSHIP HANDS

VANDERBILT, CULBERTSON AND GOREN

Who invented bridge? Well, there is no straightforward answer to that question, because bridge has similarities with many card games. Some authorities say that bridge is a direct descendant of the French card game, Plafond, which incorporated the idea of the auction, while others trace its ancestry to the Russian game Biritsch, which may or may not have come to Europe via India. Contract bridge developed from the earlier game of auction bridge, which is a nineteenth century refinement of whist. One thing we can be sure of is that the real advance from auction to contract bridge, the bidding, was developed and refined by Harold S. Vanderbilt (1884-1970) and several of his friends on a cruise on the SS Finland from Los Angeles to Havana in November 1925. Vanderbilt, an American millionaire, is supposed to have sat down at a card table at the beginning of the cruise and said, 'Gentlemen, let me show you a new game. It may interest you.' From that one table, the game developed rapidly, but it took the marketing skills of another American, Ely Culbertson, to bring the game to international popularity.

Culbertson was an American born in Romania in 1891. In 1923 he married Josephine Murphy, a leading auction bridge player, and both Culbertsons soon became very involved in Vanderbilt's new game, contract bridge. In 1930, Culbertson published *The Contract Bridge Blue Book*, in which he introduced a simple bidding system which quickly became the standard for all bidding in the United States. In

Britain, they did things differently, as usual, preferring to play what has become known as natural bridge, with no artificial conventions at all. Culbertson challenged Great Britain, in the person of Lt. Col. Walter Buller, to a match in September 1930, to prove the efficacy of Culbertson's new ideas. Culbertson and Buller were very different characters, one free and easy and perhaps rather a slob, the other a regular army officer and war hero. Culbertson often used to play with jam on his fingers, and made a point of trying to upset the British team. He was renowned for never being on time. When once he turned up at the correct hour for a rubber, he commented, 'Oh sorry, my watch must be wrong.'

The match quickly became known as 'The Match of the Century', and thanks to Culbertson's promotion of the game, bridge became a world-wide craze. As the match, over 200 rubbers, progressed at Almack's Club in London, Culbertson arranged for actors dressed up as playing cards to duplicate the moves across the Atlantic in Madison Square Garden, New York. When Culbertson's USA team won the battle by 4845 points, American enthusiasm for the game reached new heights. The defeated British squad were forced to look again at their bidding conventions (or lack of them), and it was as a direct result of this defeat that, at the Acol Bridge Club in Acol Road, Hampstead, a system of bidding was developed which has now become the British standard – the Acol System.

Culbertson went on to challenge another American, Sydney J. Lenz, to a match over 150 rubbers in 1932, to prove once again the superiority of his system, and thanks largely to the excellent play of Josephine Culbertson, who is generally reckoned to have been at least as good as her husband, his system was further vindicated. In 1936, Culbertson published his standard reference work, *Contract Bridge Complete*. Culbertson wanted to make bridge appeal to American housewives, so he decided that the best way to sell the game was on a basis of ego, sex and fear. 'We appealed to women,' wrote Culbertson in the days when male chauvinism was part of the natural order, 'and to their natural inferiority complex. Bridge was an opportunity for them to gain intellectual parity with their husbands. We worked on their fear instincts. We made it almost tantamount to shame not to play contract bridge. I also sold bridge through sex. The game brought men and women together, and I used phrases like forcing bid and approach bid because they have a connotation of sex.'

The other great American bridge expert was Charles Goren. Goren popularised the high card point system of hand valuation (invented by Milton C. Work) and wrote some 20 books on bridge, including *Winning Bridge Made Easy* in 1936. He was born in 1901 and died in April, 1991. Goren and Culbertson between them promoted bridge so that it became the most widely played table game in the world, a position that it retains today. By 1990, the Epson World Bridge Championship was contested by 88 000 people, all playing the same boards in 90 different countries, perhaps the largest organised sporting championship of all time.

NATURALS AND SCIENTISTS

Thanks to Culbertson and Goren and their successors, contract bridge is equally enjoyable to the casual player who does not want to take the game too seriously, and to the scientific player who wishes to study and master all the intricacies of the game. But the success of Culbertson's bidding techniques had one unforeseen repercussion in the development of ever more complicated bidding systems. Conventions became ever more subtle and obscure, so that even a World Master cannot get them right all the time. At the highest level, there is still a great deal of discussion about the value of a highly scientific approach to the game. I have never met a computer who could beat a bridge player with natural flair, and I do not believe that trying to model yourself on a computer is the best way to become a great bridge player.

Recently I was involved in a very interesting concept, a match between the Scientists and the Naturals. I played for the Naturals along with Tony Forrester from England, Bobby Wolff from America and Gabriel Chagas from Brazil: three of the best players in the world. The Scientists were my old golfing adversary Benito Garozzo, Billy Eisenberg, Paul Soloway and Bobby Goldman, all world champions. The Scientists were allowed to use any conventions they liked, while the only convention the Naturals were allowed to use was Blackwood to check for aces. The three matches were exceptionally close but in the end, the Scientists won two out of the three matches, although we Naturals won on overall International Match Point total. So they won the money, but we kept our pride, and the point that complicated systems and conventions are not really necessary was handsomely made.

Before the match began, we four Naturals felt we had little chance, but the match proved beyond doubt that when it comes right down to it, good or bad bridge outweighs any highly sophisticated bidding systems. This is a tremendous encouragement for the vast majority of bridge players, for whom most conventions are a closed book. The public saw the Naturals as the good guys in the white hats, and they cheered us on: they were against bids and gadgets they did not understand. They were in favour of the man who spoke plainly, over the man who spoke a complicated language.

One of the major advantages of natural bridge is that if you do not play a convention, you cannot forget it. During the match, I was playing with Tony Forrester against Garozzo and Eisenberg, and was dealt this hand:

♠ J 2   ♥ J 4 3   ♦ Q 6   ♣ K Q 9 8 6 4

Forrester opened the bidding with One No Trump, which told me he had a balanced hand, and 15-17 points — we were playing the Strong No Trump. Benito Garozzo then bid Two Diamonds, which conventionally ought to have meant he was asking Eisenberg about his major suits, but actually he had got the system wrong and was merely celebrating the fact that he held seven diamonds to the ace, and nothing much else. With my hand, nine high card points and a good club suit, I said Three No Trumps, which would be game and looked possible. Eisenberg, thinking that Garozzo had asked him to pick a major suit, looked at his hand and saw three hearts and three spades, a couple of diamonds and five clubs, enough to make him think that they could make something or defeat runs. So he doubled, which was a conventional if rather complicated way of saying to Garozzo, 'Either pass or bid one of your majors, because I've got both of them covered.' Forrester, always happy to be doubled, passed. Garozzo, still not realising that Eisenberg was asking about major suits, bid Four Diamonds, which was his way of saying that he really had rather a bad hand apart from all those diamonds. I passed, but Eisenberg now interpreted Garozzo's latest bid as an indication of a very well distributed hand, and as offering him the chance of choosing the major suit to play in. With three of each, Eisenberg bid the lower of the two. He bid Four Hearts. Tony Forrester, who if you remember, had opened One No Trump, wanted to join in the fun, and doubled the Scientists. At this point Garozzo probably realised that there had been a communication breakdown but it was too late. Everybody passed, and the Scientists discovered that they had contracted to make ten tricks in a suit in which they held a total of five cards. They went six down, a penalty of 1700. Two of the finest players in the world ended up in a totally ridiculous contract because they misunderstood each other's messages. The moral of this is that if you don't have too many understandings, you cannot have too many misunderstandings. And, especially at the lower levels, simple is best.

If you play natural bridge, your card play will improve because your brain will not be cluttered up with things to remember about the bidding. What is more, your bidding will improve. You will no longer be bidding in a straitjacket – you will be using your own judgment to evaluate the bidding conversation going on around you. One of these days we will take a team of Naturals around the world to challenge all Scientific teams, and I think that we will win at least as many as we lose. There are several tips that can help you become a better natural player.

By the way, the normal practice in rubber, or social, bridge, is to agree with your partner the convention or conventions that you will use during the game, but certainly in the early stages of your bridge development you should keep the use of conventions to a minimum.

COUNTING THE CARDS

One of the parts of card play which many people have difficulty with is counting the cards.

Here is an example in which the problem arises:

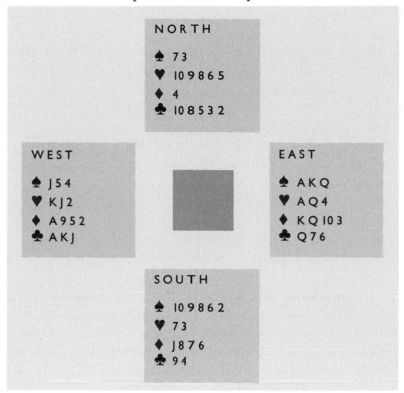

NORTH
♠ 73
♥ 109865
♦ 4
♣ 108532

WEST
♠ J54
♥ KJ2
♦ A952
♣ AKJ

EAST
♠ AKQ
♥ AQ4
♦ KQ103
♣ Q76

SOUTH
♠ 109862
♥ 73
♦ J876
♣ 94

HAND

2 6

The bidding was short but deadly:

WEST	NORTH	EAST	SOUTH
		2 NT	PASS
7 NT	PASS	PASS	PASS

South led the ten of spades. At this point Dummy's cards were put on the table and Declarer was left to STOP and consider how to play the hand. 'Thank you partner', he thought, 'that hand really is good enough to justify your leap to seven no trumps! South has led a spade, probably the top of a sequence. I have no problems in spades, hearts or clubs. But what about the jack of diamonds? That's my only potential problem. I will play the other three suits and see what happens.'

Unfortunately, nobody discarded a diamond on the way, and with four cards left to play, the diamonds, Declarer paused to decide what to do next. 'This is the moment of truth,' he thought. 'Nobody has discarded any diamonds. Let's play the king and see if anybody is void. That will tell

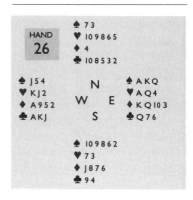

me how to play the rest of the suit.'

As you can see, neither opponent was void, and the danger card, the jack, did not appear in that first diamond trick. So, shrugging his shoulders, Declarer played a second diamond to the ace in Dummy, but when North showed out (discarded) the contract could no longer be made and went down by one. If the diamond distribution had been divided three-two between North-South, or if South's jack had been a singleton, the contract would have been made. Bad luck? Not really. Declarer made a mistake as he played. He did not count.

What Declarer did wrong in this hand was not registering what was going on in the other suits as he cashed his winners. On the third round of spades, he should have noticed that North showed out, which means that of the seven spades held by the Defenders, South had five. A mental note by Declarer. The third round of clubs would have shown him that South only had two to start with, so North had five. Another mental note by Declarer. Then by playing hearts and seeing South had only two of them Declarer could build up a picture of the pattern of South's hand: five spades, two hearts, two clubs and therefore four diamonds. Now he would know how to play the diamond suit. By starting with the king of diamonds and following with the queen, he would make the hand by finessing against South's jack of diamonds which he would know was held by South when North showed out of diamonds on the second round.

IS THE DEFENCE THAT GOOD?

Another way of swinging the odds your way a little is by remembering that when you are Declarer, more often than not Defenders will not be capable of playing highly deceptive false cards. It is just as much a mistake to overrate your opposition, as it is to underrate them. One of the tips we have discussed involves covering an honour with an honour. If a Defender does not cover your honour, it might possibly mean that he is working some great coup by ducking, but it is far more likely to mean that he has not got the relevant honour in his hand to cover with. Do not assume that when a Defender plays low smoothly when you play towards a card in your hand or in Dummy, that he is cleverly ducking. It is much more likely that he is not.

Here is an example from actual play:

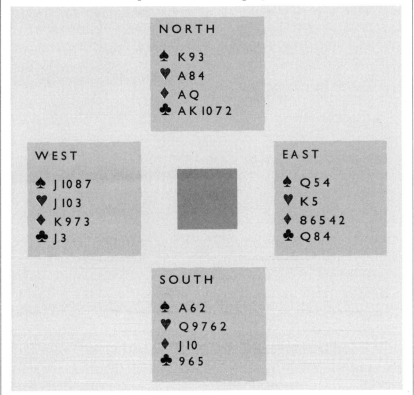

NORTH
♠ K 9 3
♥ A 8 4
♦ A Q
♣ A K 10 7 2

WEST
♠ J 10 8 7
♥ J 10 3
♦ K 9 7 3
♣ J 3

EAST
♠ Q 5 4
♥ K 5
♦ 8 6 5 4 2
♣ Q 8 4

SOUTH
♠ A 6 2
♥ Q 9 7 6 2
♦ J 10
♣ 9 6 5

HAND

The contract was Four Hearts, and West led the jack of spades which Declarer won with his king in Dummy. He then had to decide how to play the rest of the hand: the key play clearly being in the heart suit. The Declarer therefore played the ace of hearts followed by a small heart from Dummy. If East followed low to this, South intended to put up his queen of hearts, hoping East had the king. In the event, East had the king doubleton and was forced to play it on the second round. That worked because of the distribution, but I suggest that against most opposition if East on the second round had followed with a low card, Declarer (South) should think that it is more likely that East did not play the king because he did not have it, not because he was ducking. If East doesn't have the king then obviously West does, and perhaps it is West who has the doubleton, so I advise South to play low, ducking on the second round when East plays low, hoping that West started with the king doubleton.

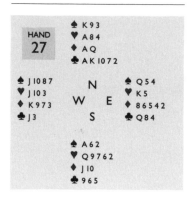

HAND 27	♠ K93
	♥ A84
	◆ AQ
	♣ AK1072

♠ J1087   ♠ Q54
♥ J103   N   ♥ K5
◆ K973 W E ◆ 86542
♣ J3   S   ♣ Q84

♠ A62
♥ Q9762
◆ J10
♣ 965

LUCK

How much of a part does luck play in top level bridge? It is not only skill that wins bridge games, as I have said before, there definitely is an element of luck, sometimes. In a World Championship (Bermuda Bowl) final a few years ago, the famous Italian *Squadro Azzura* (Blue Team) bid Seven Clubs with the following holding in clubs:

♣ A Q (Dummy)

♣ J 9 7 5 4 3 (Declarer)

The only hope of making the grand slam was for the king of clubs to be held as a doubleton by Declarer's left hand opponent. The great Giorgio Belladonna, who has played on 13 Italian Bermuda Bowl winning teams, played to his queen, which won the trick. Declarer (Belladonna) then uttered a small Italian prayer, and led out the club ace; South was forced to follow with his King and now Declarer had no losers. Italy won the title. The Americans were heard to mutter that 'God must be Italian'. But after winning all those titles on skill alone, the Italians had earned their luck.

Sometimes when I am Declarer I like to play to the gallery. Of course it does no harm to make what really is a careful calculation look like luck. I was playing in *The Sunday Times* Championship this year in a contract of Three No Trumps in hand 28 on page 103, but, I slightly overbid. West led the ace of spades, catching Dummy's singleton king, and then switched to a heart. I won the second trick in my hand and realised that I had only one entry in my hand and several finesses to take. My initial and natural reaction was to take the club finesse, but the problem was that even if it worked, I could take it only once and not again. Even if the king of clubs was doubleton it would not help me as I could make a maximum of four club tricks whether the king of clubs was doubleton or the clubs were split three-three. On the other hand if the king of diamonds was doubleton in West's hand and clubs were split three-three, I could make three diamond tricks, four club tricks and two heart tricks, my contract.

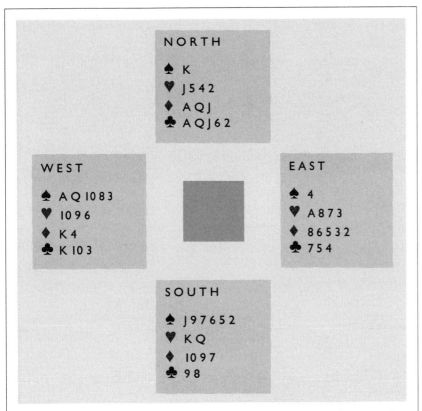

NORTH
- ♠ K
- ♥ J 5 4 2
- ♦ A Q J
- ♣ A Q J 6 2

WEST
- ♠ A Q 10 8 3
- ♥ 10 9 6
- ♦ K 4
- ♣ K 10 3

EAST
- ♠ 4
- ♥ A 8 7 3
- ♦ 8 6 5 3 2
- ♣ 7 5 4

SOUTH
- ♠ J 9 7 6 5 2
- ♥ K Q
- ♦ 10 9 7
- ♣ 9 8

So I took the diamond finesse, much to the consternation of the many spectators, but I knew my plan was the only chance. After the queen of diamonds held, I played out clubs from the Dummy and, after a few more tricks, finally came to the end of the hand where with the ace and jack of diamonds in Dummy I needed the king to fall. I had by now a complete count of the hand and knew that the king was about to fall, but wanting to savour this moment I looked up to the heavens and said, as though in prayer, 'I hope the king of diamonds comes down.' And, pretending to look away, reached for the ace of diamonds to which West reluctantly had to contribute his king of diamonds. There was a delighted roar from the audience who exclaimed about my devilish luck. It would be true to say that I enjoyed the moment, but it was actually one more example of how experts make their own luck.

In a recent World Championship final West held these cards:

♠ Q 9 6 2   ♥ A Q 9 4 2   ♦ 7   ♣ K 8 3

* North-South were playing the Western Cue Bid Convention. The Three Heart bid showed a solid suit somewhere and requested South to bid Three No Trumps if he had a heart stopper.

† Redouble was also conventional! North was telling South that he was minimum for his bid and was doubtful about the final contract! (Welcome to the twilight zone!)

HAND

The bidding had been vigorous and interesting:

WEST	NORTH	EAST	SOUTH
1 ♥	3 ♥*	PASS	3 NT
PASS	PASS	DOUBLE	PASS
PASS	REDOUBLE†	PASS	PASS
PASS			

So the final contract was Three No Trumps Redoubled, with South as Declarer. West had to find a lead. His partner had said nothing throughout the auction except to double the Three No Trumps bid, but that gave no clue as to which suit he wanted led. His own suit, hearts, was obviously controlled by South and so the choice was between a club and a spade, but which? It was highly probable that the world championship hinged on his choice. What would you have led?

Look at the full hand below.

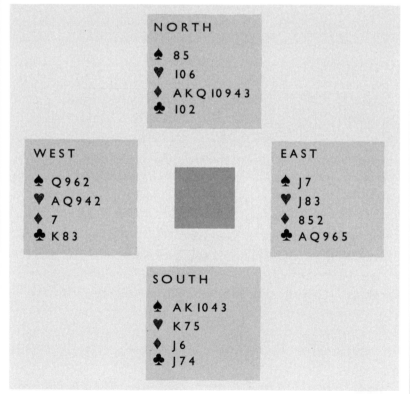

The player in question actually led a spade and the Declarer made nine tricks for a score of 950. A club lead would have meant that North-South went six down and a score of 2200 against them. And a gold medal for West!

So, as you can see, if a club is led the defence can take the first ten tricks in clubs and hearts. Lead any other suit and the contract is made. Deciding on a club lead would have been almost as much luck as good judgment, so it would be fair to say that luck plays a part in bridge, just as in any game except, perhaps, chess.

GETTING THERE

I have tried to give you a flavour of how colourful and fascinating bridge is, and I include here a hand which shows how delicate and variable the game can be. I want you to consider how you would bid a particular pair of hands that I like to use on beginners and experienced players alike. Before you look at the hands, you should know that a mathematician told me once that there were over 128 thousand million billion billion billion (yes, really) possible different combinations of cards and bids at bridge. And after playing as much bridge as I have, I believe him. You are South on this hand:

HAND

30

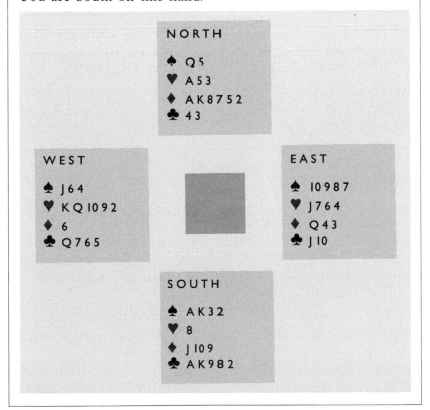

NORTH

♠ Q 5
♥ A 5 3
♦ A K 8 7 5 2
♣ 4 3

WEST

♠ J 6 4
♥ K Q 10 9 2
♦ 6
♣ Q 7 6 5

EAST

♠ 10 9 8 7
♥ J 7 6 4
♦ Q 4 3
♣ J 10

SOUTH

♠ A K 3 2
♥ 8
♦ J 10 9
♣ A K 9 8 2

HAND 30	♠ Q 5
	♥ A 5 3
	♦ A K 8 7 5 2
	♣ 4 3

♠ J 6 4	**N**	♠ 10 9 8 7
♥ K Q 10 9 2	**W E**	♥ J 7 6 4
♦ 6	**S**	♦ Q 4 3
♣ Q 7 6 5		♣ J 10

	♠ A K 3 2
	♥ 8
	♦ J 10 9
	♣ A K 9 8 2

How should you bid the two hands?

As an experiment I arranged that the hands were bid by four different partnerships. Here they are:

TABLE ONE		TABLE TWO	
SOUTH	NORTH	SOUTH	NORTH
1 ♣	1 ♦	1 ♣	2 ♦
1 ♠	2 ♦	2 ♠	3 NT
2 ♥	3 NT	6 ♦	PASS
PASS			

TABLE THREE		TABLE FOUR	
SOUTH	NORTH	SOUTH	NORTH
(Zia)	(beginner)	(Zia)	(Michele)
1 ♣	1 ♦	1 ♣	1 ♦
1 ♠	2 ♦	1 ♠	2 ♥
6 ♦	PASS	4 ♦	4 NT
		5 ♥	5 NT
		6 ♥	7 ♦
		PASS	

Three No Trumps would normally go down because the opponents' diamonds are distributed three-one, with West holding three diamonds to the queen. Six Diamonds is in fact the right contract on the combined hands. On table one, North's Two Diamonds on the second round is too weak. The correct bid is Two Hearts to force partner to game. (This bid of Two Hearts is called fourth suit forcing. Bidding the fourth suit acts both as an enquiry and simultaneously forces partner to game). As I said, Three No Trumps turns out to be a contract that normally would not be made, because of the diamond distribution. On table two, North's initial response of Two Diamonds is excellent. But Three No Trumps is bit precipitous. South bid a direct Six Diamonds, which probably astonished North but was actually a good bid. North correctly passed, and the contract made.

For the experiment I bid this hand twice myself, both times as South, once with a beginner and once with Michele Handley of the English Ladies team.

On table three, my partner also underbid with Two Diamonds just as we had seen earlier. This is a common

error made by beginners, choosing the correct suit, but the wrong level. After my opening One Club bid, he rightly told me he preferred diamonds by bidding One Diamond, but after One Spade the Two Diamond response was far too weak suggesting the partscore zone, not the game zone, which he should have been thinking about. As I said before, I prefer Two Hearts, an artificial force. My Six Diamond bid was in fact, a gamble which just happened to land on its feet. By luck we had arrived at the right contract.

When I bid with Michele, we possibly overbid our hands, landing in Seven Diamonds which was destined to fail, but which was by no means a terrible contract, and on the way we found out a great deal about what the partnership held. Her Two Hearts on the second round was a forcing bid saying, 'I like my hand. Give me some more information.' I jumped to Four Diamonds, her suit, to show extras, and she in turn used the Blackwood Convention, Four No Trumps, to ask me how many aces I held. My reply, Five Hearts, told her I had two, so she knew that between us we had four. A little slam was on, but what about a grand slam? Five No Trumps, more Blackwood, asked me about my kings. My reply, Six Hearts, told her I had two of them as well, so she bid Seven Diamonds, not unreasonably, hoping the diamonds were solid. As in that hand, it often happens in bridge that lesser players do better on a hand than experts. It's all part of the fun.

In the course of the various auctions, the four pairs made a total of sixteen quite different bids, in all five denominations. Two of the pairs ended up in the very makeable contract of Six Diamonds, one stretched to bid a grand slam, and the fourth, who made the safest bid on paper, Three No Trumps, had little chance on the actual layout. This infinite variety, this multitude of choices, the pain of failure and the joy of success are all part of the endless fascination of bridge. There is no 'right' answer, no constantly correct solution to a problem, no perfect bid, no card that can be played only one way. The difference and variety of play and styles makes bridge complicated but it also makes it infinitely absorbing. And you can learn a lot about both of your opponents by their

A TIP FROM OMAR SHARIF

'The fascination, the magic, the mystery of bridge is very difficult to explain, but one of its attractions is the fact that you can never reach perfection. In every sort of human endeavour you can get to the point where you think that you can't do much better. In chess, for example, there are only 64 squares, and although the combinations are enormous, you see the same game played over and over again. This does not happen in bridge. However good you become there is always more to learn, the games are always different. There is no routine, you can't get bored. Every time you play different opponents, you have to work out their psychology, what they are thinking and what they are doing. The magic of bridge is this continual exploration of your opponents, where there is no perfection.'

styles of bidding.

To illustrate, take a look at this hand:

♠ K 9 7 5 4   ♥ A 10 9 8 7 3   ♦ 8 4   ♣ –

Your partner bids One Spade. What would you do?

There are countless possible answers. I have listed ten below together with my idea of the personality traits which the bids reveal. Make your bid and then see what kind of person you are.

1 Pass. <u>The Suicide Merchant.</u> Although this could work out brilliantly if opponents keep bidding, this bid is made by a player with suicidal tendencies because if the opponents pass the hand out, his partner will kill him.

2 Two Clubs. <u>Crazy Genius.</u> Stealing the opponents' suit before they bid clubs. A screw loose but a flash of genius.

3 Two Hearts. <u>Scientist.</u> Carefully exploring the scientific route. Describing his hand to his partner.

4 Two Spades. <u>Tactician.</u> Hoping to get doubled at a later stage, if that stage ever comes. (Probably a cousin of Crazy Genius).

5 Three Spades. <u>Pessimist.</u> Expecting everything to go badly. He's underbidding.

6 Four Clubs. <u>Super Scientist.</u> Describing club shortage with pinpoint accuracy.

7 Four Spades. <u>Mr Practical.</u> 'I'm sure we'll make it.'

8 Five Spades. <u>Recent Divorcee</u> (my favorite). In between wives. He's not sure whether to go forwards or backwards.

9 Six Spades. <u>The Optimist.</u> 'Maybe we'll make it, if we're lucky.'

10 Seven Spades. <u>The Psycho.</u> Undoubted psychopathic tendencies. Requires psychiatric help. Do not introduce to the suicide merchant.

Well what did you bid?

THE MYSTERY OF BRIDGE

Writers have always been at a loss for the right words to define the fascination of bridge and I am no exception. But the other day when I watched a young boy playing this hand (he was South), I almost found them:

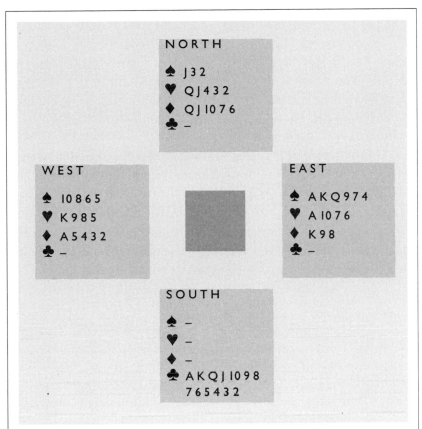

NORTH
- ♠ J32
- ♥ QJ432
- ♦ QJ1076
- ♣ –

WEST
- ♠ 10865
- ♥ K985
- ♦ A5432
- ♣ –

EAST
- ♠ AKQ974
- ♥ A1076
- ♦ K98
- ♣ –

SOUTH
- ♠ –
- ♥ –
- ♦ –
- ♣ AKQJ1098 765432

As he picked up his cards and realised that he had been dealt a dream hand, the best hand he had ever seen or would ever hold, all thirteen clubs, the expression on his face was magical. We all know that bridge players are not supposed to betray anything about their hand by their facial expression, but not surprisingly the excitement was too much, and a broad grin spread across his face. He knew he could make a grand slam, and he was unable to hold back his eagerness and his anticipation.

The bidding was as follows:

SOUTH	WEST	NORTH	EAST
7 ♣	PASS	PASS	DOUBLE
REDOUBLE	PASS	PASS	7 ♠

East Doubled initially because of her attractive hand, but on hearing the Redouble she decided that South must have all thirteen clubs, or the double would not have been so firmly and eagerly redoubled. So instead of letting him play the hand, she bid Seven Spades, and South lost his chance of playing the hand of a lifetime. East-West went down of course, but that result was better than a grand slam redoubled against them, which would have given North-South 560 points below the line and 1200 above the line, including bonuses of 200 for trump honours and the insult of being doubled. If South had not redoubled, he would have made his grand slam.

In the space of a few minutes, that young boy went through the gamut of emotions, from elation to disappointment and despair. He came out of it even more captivated by this deviously simple game of bridge. Somewhere in this story lies the fun, the excitement, the magic and the mystery of bridge, and I hope that you, too, will discover the magic just as that young boy did.

The objective at bridge is to win the rubber. The rubber is decided on the best of three games and once a partnership has won one game (100 points or more), that partnership is said to be vulnerable. This affects some of the scores.

POINTS BELOW THE LINE

All points towards game and rubber are scored below the line. One hundred points or more below the line win the game. Points are scored according to the number of tricks contracted and made.

SUIT	CONTRACT SIZE						
	One	Two	Three	Four	Five	Six	Seven
No Trumps	40	70	100	130	160	190	220
Major suits ♠ ♥	30	60	90	120	150	180	210
Minor Suits ♦ ♣	20	40	60	80	100	120	140

All totals are doubled when the contract is doubled, and quadrupled when the contract is redoubled. Thus Three Clubs doubled and successfully made would yield 120 points below the line, enough for game. One Heart redoubled and made would also yield 120 points below the line.

Once 100 points have been scored by one partnership or the other, the game is over. Points over 100 cannot be carried over to the next game. A contract yielding 210 points below the line still only wins one game.

If a contract is not made, no points are scored below the line.

POINTS ABOVE THE LINE

Overtricks are tricks made above and beyond the contract amount. So if the contract is Two Clubs, and your partnership makes nine tricks, ie one more than contracted, you have made one overtrick, which is scored above the line. If the contract is undoubled, the score above the line is calculated in exactly the same way as the score below the line. In other words, one overtrick in Clubs scores 20 points above the line as well as 40 points below the line for making the contract. Three overtricks in spades would score 90 points above the line.

If the contract is doubled, each non-vulnerable overtrick is valued at 100 points, regardless of suit. If the contract is doubled, and the Declarer's side is vulnerable, the value above the line for each overtrick doubled is 200 points. Redoubling the Double would mean that overtricks would be worth 200 each for a non-vulnerable partnership, and 400 each vulnerable.

<u>Undertricks</u> are tricks by which Declarer falls short of his contract. If the contract is for Three Clubs, and Declarer only wins eight tricks, he has gone down one trick. Each undertrick scores points for the defence above the line as follows: 50 points for each trick if the Declarer is not vulnerable, and 100 points per trick vulnerable. If the contract has been doubled, then the scoring is 100 points for the first undertrick, and 200 points for each subsequent undertrick against a non-vulnerable partnership and 200 points for the first undertrick against a vulnerable partnership, and 300 after that. Redoubling simply doubles all these figures.

<u>Bonuses</u> are awarded for three different achievements: making a slam, winning a rubber, and making a doubled contract.

The bonuses for making a slam are as follows:

BIDDING AND MAKING A SMALL SLAM (12 TRICKS):

non-vulnerable	– 500 points
vulnerable	– 750 points

BIDDING AND MAKING A GRAND SLAM (13 TRICKS):

non-vulnerable	– 1000 points
vulnerable	– 1500 points

<u>The bonuses for winning a rubber are:</u> 500 points if your opponents have won one game and 700 points if they have won none. If you have to stop before a rubber is completed (for example, if dinner is ready or a fire has

broken out in a Toronto hotel) 300 bonus points are awarded to any side that has made a game. If only one side has a partscore in an unfinished game, it scores a further 50 points.

The bonus for making a doubled or a redoubled contract is: 50 points, regardless of vulnerability. These points are additional to any overtrick scores which are also won on the hand.

NB: Some of the scoring at duplicate bridge is a little different, but it is only a variation on the same theme.

Honours are still awarded points in rubber bridge, although the system is not in use in duplicate (tournament) bridge. When a player holds all five trump honours (A K Q J 10) in his own hand, or all four aces if the contract is in No Trumps, a bonus of 150 points is awarded. If a player holds four of the five trump honours, he earns a bonus of 100. Either side can score honours, although it would be a very poor partnership that bid to a contract in a suit in which a Defender held all the honours.

If the game is being played for money, all figures, above and below the line, are added up and the losers pay on the basis of the difference between the two total scores. It is normal practice to set stakes at a rate per 100 points and to work to the nearest hundred. Thus, 840 is eight points, but 870 is nine.

SCORECARD EXAMPLE

This is how the scorecard would look at the end of a rubber in which:

● you and your partner (We) had bid and made Three No Trumps on the first hand – 100 below the line;

● your opponents bid and made Two Hearts with one overtrick on the second hand – 30 above and 60 below the line;

● your opponents bid and made One Club on the third hand – 20 below the line;

● you and your partner bid and made Two Spades Doubled on the fourth and final hand of this rubber – 120 below and 50 above the line. This is the last hand of the rubber because you and your partner had made the first two games, and had therefore made rubber.

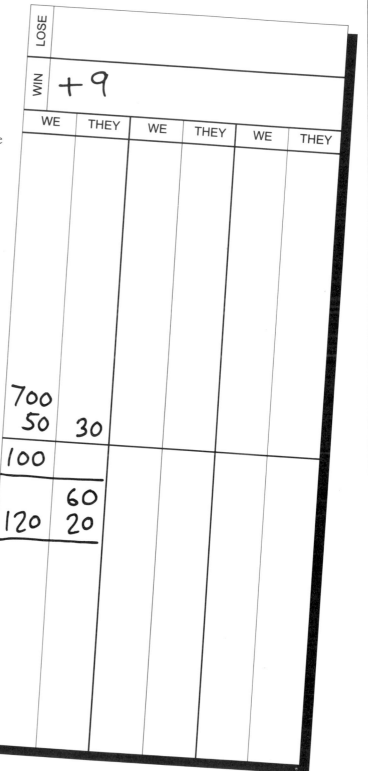

Above the line: In bridge scoring, the place where overtricks, bonus and penalty points are written.

Acol: A system of bidding, named after the road in North London which contained the bridge club in which the bidding method was pioneered.

Artificial bid: A bid which does not mean that the bidder wants to play in the contract he bids but which contains some other message. For example, in the Stayman Convention, Two Clubs does not necessarily imply wanting to play in clubs. (See Stayman Convention).

Auction: The process of bidding for the contract for the hand, which begins with the dealer and proceeds clockwise round the table.

Balanced hand: A hand with any of the following distribution of cards: 4-3-3-3; 4-4-3-2; 5-3-3-2.

Below the line: In bridge scoring, the place where points towards game are written.

Bid: A number, from one to seven, and a denomination (no trumps, spades, hearts, diamonds, clubs), which is an undertaking to win at least a certain number of tricks in that denomination. The bid is also used to give partner information about your hand.

Blackwood: An artificial bid of Four No Trumps when looking for a slam contract, to ask partner how many aces he holds. At the five level, the convention can be used to find kings.

Blocking: A play to attempt to prevent the running of an established suit.

Bonus: Points awarded for making rubber in two or three games, for bidding and making a slam, etc.

Book: The first six tricks, which are taken for granted in any bid, therefore a bid of say, Three Clubs, implies the intention to take nine tricks, and so on.

Contract: The number of tricks and the denomination suggested by the bid. Four Spades, for example, means that you undertake to win ten tricks (six for the book plus four bid) with spades as trumps.

Controls: Controlling cards: aces and kings, or a shortage in a suit other than trumps.

Convention: An artificial bid which, by agreement or understanding between partners, serves to convey a meaning other than the one that would be attributed to it by the opponents in the absence of an explanation. (For example, *see* Blackwood or Stayman).

Count: A signal by one Defender that tells his partner how many cards in any suit he holds. The normal method is to play a high card followed by a low card to show that the Defender holds an even number of cards at the time of playing the first card. The other way round means an odd number.

Cue Bid: A bid in a suit in which the bidder does not want to play. The Cue Bid usually shows the ace or a control in the bid suit.

Cut: At the start of a session, the four players cut for partners. The two players who cut the highest cards partner each other. The player who cut the highest card deals the first hand.

Declarer: The player who first called the denomination (the suit or no trumps) in which the hand is to be played.

Defence: *See* Defenders below.

Defenders: The partners who are attempting to defeat Declarer's contract are the Defenders. The opening bid is always made by the Defender on Declarer's left.

Denomination: The suit (or no trumps) in which the contract is played.

Discard: A card played by a player who has no cards in the suit led.

Distribution: The number of cards in each suit held in a hand. The shape of the hand.

Double: A bid whose effect is to increase the size of the penalty if the opponents' contract fails. This bid can be construed as either a penalty double or a takeout double, depending on the agreement in the partnership.

Doubleton: Two cards in any suit is a doubleton. This is comparatively common and of less strategic value than a singleton or a void.

Draw Trumps: When Declarer plays trumps in order to remove trumps from the opposing partnership.

Down: Failure to make a contracted bid.

Duck: A strategic play: to play low from a suit when you could play a high card. Deliberately not to try to win a trick you could have won, or tried to win.

Dummy: Declarer's partner, who lays out his 13 cards face up on the table, opposite his partner, after the opening lead.

Dummy points: Points used when you think you are going to be Dummy, support your partner's choice of trump suit and are happy to bid to contract. A void = 5 points; a singleton = 3 points; a doubleton = 1 point.

Duplicate bridge: A form of bridge in which all contestants play the same series of hands. The format used in most tournaments.

Entry: A winning card which allows the Declarer or the defence to move from one hand to the other.

Finesse: Trying to win a trick with a high card when you know a higher card is held by your opponents. The question is – where?

Forcing bid: A bid that insists that partner keeps the bidding open and does not pass. An opening of Two in any suit is a forcing bid.

Game: One hundred or more points scored below the line gives game. Two games must be won to take the rubber.

Grand slam: A contract to make 13 tricks in any denomination. In other words to take all the tricks.

Guard: *See* Cover.

Hand: Either the cards held in one's own hand or the collective noun for all four hands.

High card points: A way of valuing the strength of the hand by awarding points: ace = 4, king = 3, queen = 2 and jack = 1. Sometimes known as Milton Work points after the developer of the idea.

Hold up: To delay playing a winner. Any play which does so.

Honours: The four aces are the honours in no trumps. The A, K, Q, J, 10 are the honours in a suit.

IMP: Abbreviation for International Match Point. (A form of scoring, particularly frequently used in team events at duplicate bridge.)

Informative discard: A discard which tells your partner what suit you are happy in, or unhappy about. (*See* Signals.)

Jump raise: A bid two levels higher in the same suit as partner, often indicating a good hand.

Jump shift bid: This bid is the same as a jump, but is in a different suit from partner's.

Loser: Any card which is not certain to win a trick.

Length points: Points scored for every suit of five cards or more: 5 card suit = 1 point; 6 card suit = 2 points; 7 card suit = 3 points; 8 card suit = 4 points. Some players score one point for every card above four in a suit, so: 9 card suit = 5 points; 10 card suit = 6 points; 11 card suit = 7 points; 12 card suit = 8 points; 13 card suit = 9 points.

Major suits: Spades and hearts are the major suits.

Minor suits: Diamonds and clubs are the minor suits.

No bid: An alternative way of saying 'Pass'. (In England the former is standard language, in America the latter).

No Trumps: A contract in no trumps means exactly what it says: no suit is trumps. It is ranked higher than spades on the bidding ladder.

Non-vulnerable: A partnership, or both partnerships, when they have not yet made game within the rubber being played.

Opener: The player who makes the first bid in the auction. The player with the right to make the first bid is the dealer, but if he passes, then the Opener is the player who actually makes the first bid other than a pass.

Opening values: Enough points to open the bidding: generally accepted to be at least 12 high card points.

Overcall: To make a bid after the opposition has opened the bidding.

Overtake: Play a card higher than the one already played by your side, even though the original card might well have won the trick.

Overtricks: Extra tricks made, over and above the number contracted for.

Overtrump: Play a trump on a trick higher than the trump already played on the trick.

Palooka: A very bad bridge player.

Partscore: A contract for less than game.

Pass: To make no bid. After three consecutive passes, the auction is closed (except on the opening round of the auction when the player fourth in hand may bid).

Penalty: Points given to the defence if the Declarer fails to make the contract.

Penalty Double: A double which will increase the size of the penalty if the opponents' contract fails. All doubles of no trump bids are construed as penalty doubles, whether bid in the first round or later. (*See also* Takeout Double).

Pigeon: A player who is seen by the others at the table, especially when playing for money, as the likely loser.

Points: Values given to the high cards (*see* high card points) and to the length of suits, (*see* length points) to evaluate the strength of a hand.

Pre-emptive bid: A bid made at a higher level than the player's points indicate, as a defensive tactic to limit your opponents' room for manœuvre.

Premium points: Extra points, scored above the line, given to the team that bids and makes a slam contract or game, or to the team that defeats their opponents' contract.

Promoting winners: Forcing out your opponents' higher cards in any suit so as to set up winners for your side.

Psychic (bluff) bid: A bid which is intended to disrupt and confuse the opposition by representing that you hold values or distribution which you do not actually possess.

Raise: Support your partner's denomination at a higher level.

Redouble: A bid after your opponent's double, which further increases the points at stake.

Responder: Opener's partner.

Response: A reply to partner's opening bid.

Revoke: Players must follow suit. If a player does not follow suit when he can, he has revoked. The penalty is the transfer of two tricks to the other side, or only one if the trick in which the revoke occurred was lost by the revoker anyway.

Rubber: The best of three games. The first team to win two games achieves a bonus.

Ruff: To play a trump on the lead of a side-suit.

Ruff and a sluff: A trick in which the card led is of a suit in which both Declarer and Dummy are void. Declarer therefore ruffs from one hand and plays a sluff (discard) from the other.

Sacrifice bidding: Winning an auction for a contract you know you are unlikely to achieve, to prevent your opponents winning the auction and possibly the game.

Shape: The distribution of cards by denomination in a

hand. (*See* balanced hand.) All shapes other than balanced hands are described as irregular or unbalanced.

Shift: A term used to mean to return a suit other than the one led by your partner.

Showing out: Discarding when a suit is led which shows you have no more cards in that suit.

Side-Suit: Any suit that is not the trump suit.

Sign-off bid: A bid to tell your partner when to stop.

Signals: Cards played which signal to partner what suit he should lead, retain or discard.

Singleton: To start a hand with only one card in any suit is called a singleton.

Small slam: The bidding and making of twelve tricks.

Splinter bid: A conventional bid, showing support for partner's suit. It is a jump bid promising a shortage (a singleton or a void) in the bid suit.

Squeeze: A play which forces an opponent to discard a winner, or to unguard a suit.

Stayman: A bidding convention named after the American Sam Stayman. In response to a One No Trump bid, partner may bid Two Clubs in order to see whether there is a four-four fit in a major suit. A response of Two Diamonds denies a four card major suit.

Stiff: A singleton.

Stop: A card which will prevent your opponents reeling out their winners in that suit.

STOP: An acronym standing for Stop to consider your goal, Tally your winners and losers, Organise your plan and Put your plan into action. Try to STOP before embarking on playing any hand, whether as Declarer or Defender.

Stranded winners: Winners left in a hand into which there is no entry.

Takeout double: A low level double, practically always bid on the first or second round of bidding, to ask partner to bid his best suit. If the next opponent to speak does not bid it is a forcing bid, to be passed only when your trump holding dictates it.

Tenace: A combination of honours from which one card in the middle is missing.

Touching suits: Suits which are ranked next to each other, for example diamonds and clubs.

Tournament bridge: *See* Duplicate.

Trick: Four cards played, one by each player. The winner of the trick is the person who plays the highest card in the suit led, or if one or more players cannot follow suit, the person who takes the trick with the highest trump.

Trick points: Points awarded for making a contract, scored below the line.

Trump suit: The suit named in the final contract.

Undertricks: The tricks by which Declarer falls short of achieving the contract.

Void: A suit which is completely absent from a hand.

Vulnerable: When a partnership makes game, it becomes vulnerable. The points penalties for failing to achieve subsequent contracts are much higher for a partnership which is vulnerable. Both partnerships can be vulnerable at the same time.

Weakness take out: Responding to partner's One No Trump bid by bidding Two in any suit except clubs. This shows weakness and partner should not rebid.

Western Cue Bid: An overcall of Three of your right hand opponent's suit. It tells your partner that you have a solid side-suit and requests partner to bid Three No Trumps if he has a stop in Declarer's suit.

Winner: A card which will certainly win the trick when played.

Yarborough: A hand with no honours.

Zone: Partscore, game or slam – the three zones to aim for according to the strength of the cards in the partnership.

INDEX

The following pages can be cut out and taken with you for quick reference when playing bridge. They will help you calculate your high card points, remind you of the points required for different bids, translate the language of the most common bidding conventions and provide a quick guide to scoring.

SUIT RANKING & BALANCED HANDS

The Major Suits = ♠ and ♥
The Minor Suits = ♦ and ♣
Suit rankings = Alphabetically in descending order: Spades, Hearts, Diamonds and Clubs
Balanced hand patterns:
    4-3-3-3, 4-4-3-2 and 5-3-3-2.

COUNTING YOUR POINTS

HCPs (high card points)
There are 40 HCPs in a pack of cards, made up as follows:
    Ace = 4, King = 3, Queen = 2 and Jack = 1 (in each suit)

LENGTH POINTS

You may score the following points for length in a suit, but be careful to separate these points from HCPs when calculating which zone your partnership is to play in.
(*see* The Three Zones)
5 card suit = 1, 6 card suit = 2,
7 card suit = 3, 8 card suit = 4,
and some people continue on:
9 card suit = 5, 10 card suit = 6,
11 card suit = 7, 12 card suit = 8,
13 card suit = 9.

DUMMY POINTS

When your partner has bid a suit in which you have a fit you can count the following extra points for shortages in a side suit:
    Void = 5,
    Singleton = 3 and
    Doubleton = 1.

(Obviously a shortage in your partner's chosen suit *does not* count for any points)

Both the above categories can only serve as guidelines rather than hard and fast rules.

THE THREE ZONES

Partscore Zone –
    partnership points required = under 26.
Game Zone –
    partnership points required = 26-32.
Slam Zone –
    partnership points required = 33-36 (small slam) or 37+ (grand slam).

POINTS REQUIRED TO BID

The following are generally accepted and provide a guideline, but again there are no hard and fast rules:

0-5   Do not open nor respond to a non-forcing opening from your partner. (However, if partner uses a forcing bid, you must reply).

6-11   You have enough points to respond to your partner's opening bid, but not to insist on playing in game.

Pre-emptive bid

6-10   6 + cards and a reasonable holding in one suit. 3 of your long suit (subject to discretion depending on whether you are vulnerable).

Non-forcing bids

10-12   mini One No Trump.

12-21   opening bid in a suit, or an overcall. You have enough points to play in game if your partner opens the bidding.

12+   and all three suits, except opponent's bid suit, covered – Double (takeout).

12-14   and a balanced hand – One No Trump (weak).

15+   called over your opponent's weak No Trump opening – Double (penalty).

15-17   One No Trump (strong).

20-22   and a balanced hand – Two No Trumps.

Forcing bids

17-23   Assuming you have at least one long suit and good playing strength (eight or more playing tricks), Two of a suit (except clubs). Otherwise open at the one level.

23+   Two Clubs.

23-24   and a balanced hand – open Two Clubs and rebid Two No Trumps.

25-26   and a balanced hand – open Two Clubs and rebid Three No Trumps.

CONVENTIONAL BIDS

The Blackwood Convention

In the game or slam zone. Use to discover how many aces and kings the partnership holds:

Questioning partner –
 4NT = how many aces?

Answering partner –
 5♣ = none (or 4)
 5♦ = 1
 5♥ = 2
 5♠ = 3

Questioning partner –
 5NT = how many kings?

Answering partner –
 6♣ = none (or 4)
 6♦ = 1
 6♥ = 2
 6♠ = 3

The Stayman Convention

In the partscore, game or slam zone, to establish which major suit, if any, the partnership has a four-four fit in:

Opening partner –
 INT = a balanced hand.

Questioning partner –
 2♣ = tell me in which major suit you have at least four cards because I have at least four in one of them.

Answering partner –
 2♦ = I have neither four cards in hearts or spades.
 2♥ = I have four hearts, and maybe four spades.
 2♠ = I have four spades. I do not have four hearts.

The Two Club Opener

In the game or slam zone. To try to establish the correct suit and simultaneously convey the message of an excellent hand:

Opening partner –
 2♣ = I have at least 23 points. Tell me about your hand. (This is a forcing bid so partner must answer)

Answering partner –
 2♦ = My hand is awful. Sorry, (generally 0-7 points). 2 of a major suit or 3 of a minor suit indicate your best suit.

The Two of a Suit Opener

(This is a natural bid, but forcing for one round, showing a hand of power and quality).

Answering partner –
 2NT = I have a bad hand. All other responses are natural and game forcing.

BOOK + TRICKS FOR CONTRACTS

Book = 6 tricks
So the number of tricks to be made will always be 7+.
If the contract is in:
1 of a suit = 7 tricks (partscore call)
2 of a suit = 8 tricks (partscore call)
3 of a suit = 9 tricks (game call in no trumps)
4 of a suit = 10 tricks (game call in major suits)
5 of a suit = 11 tricks (game call in minor suits)
6 of a suit = 12 tricks (small slam)
7 of a suit = 13 tricks (grand slam)

SCORING

Points below the line
GAME = at least 100 points.
ONLY partscore or game points are scored below the line.

SUIT	CONTRACT SIZE						
	One	Two	Three	Four	Five	Six	Seven
No Trumps	40	70	100	130	160	190	220
Major suits ♠ ♥	30	60	90	120	150	180	210
Minor Suits ♦ ♣	20	40	60	80	100	120	140

Points above the line
Overtricks
Ordinary overtricks –
   suit value as above.
Doubled, non-vulnerable –
   100 per trick.
Doubled, vulnerable –
   200 per trick.
Redoubled, non-vulnerable –
   200 per trick.
Redoubled, vulnerable –
   400 per trick.

Undertricks
Ordinary undertricks –
   suit value as above.
non-vulnerable –
   50 per trick.
vulnerable –
   100 per trick.
Doubled, non-vulnerable –
   100 first trick,
   200 subsequent tricks.
Doubled, Vulnerable –
   200 first trick,
   300 subsequent tricks.
Redoubled, non-vulnerable –
   200 first trick,
   400 subsequent tricks.
Redoubled, vulnerable –
   400 first trick.
   600 subsequent tricks.

Bonus points
For the insult to a partnership who
make a doubled or redoubled contract –
   50.
Small slam, non-vulnerable –
   500.
Small slam, vulnerable –
   750.
Grand slam, non-vulnerable –
   1000.
Grand slam, vulnerable –
   1500.
Rubber in two games –
   700.
Rubber in three games –
   500.
Honours (A K Q J 10 in the trump
suit or all four aces in no trumps) –
   150.
Any four or five of the honours of
the trump suit –
   100.